Advance Praise for
BEAUTIFUL SINGING

Stan Felix isn't just a singing guy. Above and beyond his many years of exceptional leadership as a singing-actor and teacher, his broad life-experience has led him to a practical pedagogy that is more accessible than most. The act of forming and supporting shapes and sounds to create what we know as good singing should be a simple, soul-driven activity, yet it is often blown up into intense techno-processes that can easily drive one away from the very reason singing should happen at all. This book will help the singing-actor become a natural communicator of this great art.
—ROBERT SWEDBERG, ASSOCIATE PROFESSOR OF MUSIC EMERITUS, UNIVERSITY OF MICHIGAN

Stanford Felix's *Beautiful Singing* contains invaluable information for the beginning voice student, the seasoned professional, and every level in between. His approach is both scholarly and personal and should find a place on every singer's bookshelf.
—Neal Goren, Founding Artistic Director, Gotham Chamber Opera; Associate Professor at Mannes College, The New School for Music, and author of *Beyond the Aria*

This book is a must for every vocal coach, teacher, and serious singer and will sit on my piano or desk for reference. Stanford Felix has written an intense conversation on the art of singing that contains valuable information packed into every paragraph. *Beautiful Singing* may become the next must for every vocal pedagogy class.
—Robin Jensen, Opera Program Music Director and Instructor of Collaborative Piano in the Vocal Arts, University of Central Florida

Advance Praise for
BEAUTIFUL SINGING

An informative and authentic resource for teachers and students alike. Bravissimo!
—Wendy Zaro Mullins, Associate Professor of Voice, University of Minnesota School of Music

With his thorough guide, Stanford Felix has made a significant contribution to the community of serious singers and their teachers. The aural experience of vocal sound is evanescent and hard to measure. The process of producing it is beset with many intangibles. So it is no wonder that this field of human endeavor has had, for centuries, an aura of mystery and frustrating inexactitude. . . . Perhaps the biggest overall challenge is to bridge the gaps between inner feelings, aural imagination, bodily self-perceptions, emotional connections, and actual produced musical utterances.

Dr. Felix has managed to grapple with all these different aspects both separately and in conjunction. . . . For me this is the unique strength of this exhaustive volume; at every point the reader is reminded to be aware of the final goal: integration of means and ends. Felix eschews a microscopic repetition of areas that have been over-represented in singing texts such as phonetics and pronunciation, and seeks rather to guide the reader into myriad practical ways to combine basic exploration of the different fundamentals and construction of a coherent overall technique. Throughout, he draws on his own experiences in a profoundly didactic manner.
—Jonathan Khuner, Musical Director, West Edge Opera, and former assistant conductor at San Francisco Opera, Metropolitan Opera, and Lyric Opera of Chicago

Beautiful Singing

Beautiful Singing

A Singer's Guide to Improving the Voice

STANFORD FELIX

Perfect Pitch Press

Perfect Pitch Press

Copyright © 2020 by Stanford P. Felix

Published by Perfect Pitch Press.

All rights reserved. No part of this book may be reproduced in whole or in part without written permission from the publisher, except by reviewers who may quote brief excerpts in connection with a review in a newspaper, magazine, or electronic publication; nor may any part of this book be reproduced, stored in a retrieval system, or transmitted in any form or by any means electronic, mechanical, photocopying, recording, or other, without written permission from the publisher.

Without limitation, nothing contained in this book should replace medical advice, medical visits, or recommendations from health care providers. Patients should always consult with a doctor or other health care provider for medical advice.

"Anatomy of the Human Voice" image obtained from Wikimedia Commons, JohannaO14 / CC BY-SA, https://commons.wikimedia.org/wiki/File:Hoarseness_image.jpg

Excerpts from "Qualifications for Teachers of Singing" by the American Academy of Teachers of Singing. Copyright © 2001 by the American Academy of Teachers of Singing (AATS). Reprinted by permission of AATS. All rights reserved.

"Piano Keyboard Reference" image © John Ellinger. Used with permission.

Library of Congress Cataloging-in-Publication Data is available.

ISBN: 978-0-578-80307-4 (paperback)

Interior design by Timothy Shaner, NightandDayDesign.biz

beautifulsinging.org

For my parents, Paul and Trudy Felix,
and my wife, Antonia,
with gratitude for your love and encouragement.

Contents

FOREWORD by Kevin Langan..........................1
ACKNOWLEDGMENTS..............................3
INTRODUCTION..7

1 ~ THE MIND CONNECTION..........................17
Motivation, imagery, imagination, intellectual focus, self-perception, and other mental aspects of vocal artistry.

2 ~ THE RESONANCE CONNECTION.................39
Understanding the formation, characteristics, and elements of resonance, from the singer's formant to a beautiful timbre.

3 ~ THE BREATH CONNECTION......................77
Correct management of the breath for the best support and sound, with unique exercises.

4 ~ THE LANGUAGE CONNECTION.................111
Choosing repertoire, approaching languages, using the International Phonetic Alphabet (IPA), mastering diction, and preparing texts.

5 ~ THE BODY CONNECTION........................147
Physical elements of singing, including body posture and alignment, considerations about the face and hands, and effective body warm-up exercises.

6 ~ THE TEACHER CONNECTION....................169
A guide to choosing a teacher, how to practice, vocal registers, vocal health dos and don'ts, and fixes for common vocal problems.

APPENDIX I: Vocal Disorders and Faults............... 198
APPENDIX II: Internet Resources for Singers.......... 213
BIBLIOGRAPHY 227
INDEX 233

Foreword

I first met Stanford Felix when his company, Minnesota Concert Opera, hired me to perform in its production of *The Mini Ring*, an abbreviated, one-evening version of Wagner's four-opera *Der Ring Des Nibelungen*, conducted by Jonathan Khuner and performed in the Cowles Center for Dance and the Performing Arts in Minneapolis in 2013. Everyone in the cast, which included Jay Hunter Morris, Lori Phillips, Richard Paul Fink, Philip Skinner, Sarah Heltzel, and my wife, Sally Wolf, had a marvelous time navigating this unique rendition of Wagner's masterwork under Stanford's caring and enthusiastic eye as the company's founder and artistic director. Seven years later, I was delighted to learn that he was writing a book about vocal technique.

A legitimate book on good, healthy singing technique must be based on a proven method handed down from person to person over the centuries, which results in the performer communicating successfully some part of the human condition to the listener through music. Dr. Felix's *Beautiful Singing* does just that. Giovanni Lamperti condensed many maxims of proper vocalism he gathered from working with the method that the Manuel Garcia family formulated in the eighteenth and nineteenth centuries, and which their students mastered and subsequently spread across the Western world up to the present time. Dr. Felix is a singer and veteran teacher of singing who has in this book broken down Lamperti's most important maxims into concisely explained technical concepts for the modern singer to embrace, regardless of the style of music they are undertaking, be it a classical or musical theater approach. He also touches upon maintaining good health both in the body and the voice itself, so important to finding success as a professional.

This book is a wonderful companion for the young singer who is embarking on a career with a trusted voice teacher to expand and enlighten what the student will feel in the studio. What you will read here will help you understand the sensations needed for a good, disciplined, healthy vocal technique that can last you for decades.

Kevin Langan
August 10, 2020

Kevin Langan is an American bass with a career of over 42 years, amassing nearly 1,500 performances of 92 different roles with over 70 professional opera and symphonic organizations worldwide.

Acknowledgments

There are so many people to acknowledge who have helped form my music career over the years: piano teachers, band directors, choir directors, stage directors, voice teachers, vocal coaches, composers, conductors, producers, teaching colleagues, and fellows singers. My dad and mom, Paul and Trudy Felix, were always supportive of my endeavors and encouraged me and my four brothers—Rich, Dave, Bruce, and Tony—to take up an instrument. I don't know how my parents afforded all my lessons over the years, but I will always be thankful that they believed in me and my love of music.

I am also grateful for those teachers and directors who gave of themselves wholeheartedly in my studies of theater, dance, art, and literature. Under their guidance, every play, dance performance, museum visit, and novel gave me a view of the world far beyond the small South Dakota town in which I grew up.

Special thanks also go to my students. To you hundreds of private voice students, voice class students, choir students, masterclass and workshop students, and opera workshop students, thank you for sharing my love of singing and always reminding me that there is always something more to learn.

Remembering all my music associates over the years by name would be futile, but I would like to recognize many who have inspired me and left a mark on me as a musician, singer, vocal pedagogue, and teacher. Beginning with my voice teachers, most of whom are still with us, but some who have passed, thank you for your insight, musicality, professional approach, and kind interactions: Shirley Neugebauer, Milo Pietz, Grover Brown, Keith "Larry" Torkelson, Antonio Perez, Kenneth Smith, Emma Small, Armen Boyajian, Franco Iglesias, William Riley, Spiro Malas, Maitland Peters, and John Stephens. Thank you to my vocal coaches: Leon Burke III, Mark Ferrell, Kenneth Merrill, Barbara Brooks, Paul Nadler, Dale Johnson, Donna Racik, Doug Stanton, Richard Gordan, Warren Helms, Marcello Garofalo, Craig Rutenberg, Shirlee Emmons, W. Stephen Smith, Neal Goren, Robin Jensen, Lara Bolton, Miriam Charney, and Cynthia Hoffmann.

With gratitude to my conductors and choir directors: Robert Larsen, George Lawner, Philip Brunelle, Jonathan Khuner, David Gilbert, Dale Warland, Stewart Robertson, Richard Owens, Yves Abel, Gordon Ostrowski, Buck Ross, Benton Hess, Richard Cordova, John Paul Johnson, James Ralston, Stephen Hamilton, Craig Fields, Karen Keltner, and Richard Owens. Thanks also to my acting and diction teachers: Jack Wright, Rhoda Levine, Tim Ocel, Kathryn LaBouff, Robert Cowart, and Palma Toscani.

Heartfelt appreciation goes to my musician and artist friends, accompanists, and teaching colleagues: Kevin Langan, Dennis Petersen, Clifton and Bettye Ware, Lynn Trapp, Joyce Castle, Andrea Garritano, Frank Sonntag, Penny Speedy, Genaro Mendez, Pamela Hinchman, Carol Krueger, Neil Conrad, Marcia Laningham, Tricia Leines, Karol Sue Reddington, Kara Millerhagen, Marla Frees, Hugo Vera, Tyler Simpson, Christian Elser, Brendan Snook, Ben Gulley, Tina Christensen, Madalyn Staupe Traun, Gisela Corbett, Katherine Keefer, Linda Scher, Bruce Felix, Audrey Schindler, Lynn Schindler, Renate Sharp, David Frank, Alan and Myrna Comstock, Mary Veronica Sweeney, Chris Hubbard, Inci Bashar Paige, Norman Paige, Richard Elder Adams, Bernadette

Hoke, Angel Yang, David Carey, Noel Archambeault, Jeff Hodapp, Martin Cuellar, Andrew Houchins, and John (Jack) Lennon. I am especially thankful for the years of great conversation and friendship with Wendy Zaro-Mullins, Joseph and Elizabeth Mahowald, and Robin Jensen.

I am also deeply grateful to those who produced this book for Perfect Pitch Press with their talented expertise: copyeditor Thomas Pitoniak, indexer Jay Kreider, the incredible design team of Timothy Shaner and Christopher Measom, and last, but not at all least, editor Antonia Felix, my wife, whose writing career has always been an inspiration to me and whose ideas, conversations, and musical know-how contributed a great deal as I wrote this book.

Introduction

"Singing is a natural use of the voice. But to learn . . . demands training of brain and body until desire and reflex control the process. Then that which was difficult becomes easy." —Giovanni Battista Lamperti

I wrote this book as a response to my students and colleagues who have asked for an uncomplicated, to-the-point guide to good singing. Since hundreds of technically detailed scholarly books and online sources on *bel canto* (*Italian*, beautiful singing) technique are available, I saw a need to simplify the learning process by offering a concise, easy-to-understand guide of vocal techniques and fixes for the serious voice student. That was my goal, and I hope you find that I have thrown light on how to approach some of the most important and difficult aspects of vocal technique in a readable fashion. Sharing the unique ideas, fixes, and exercises I've developed and accumulated over nearly forty-five years as a professional singer and voice teacher, this book is designed to help even the most experienced singer more clearly understand certain aspects of the *bel canto* technique, the proven foundation for all styles of singing.

THE TECHNIQUE
Bel canto, a style of singing developed over nearly 450 years, emphasizes breath control, registers and range, intonation, intensity

control, and the use of the mental concept of imitation, or ear training. The student who studies this method in conjunction with conscious listening will learn to eliminate vowel distortions and reveal the tone and natural quality, or *timbre*, of the voice. The techniques and fixes spelled out in this manual, along with the student's openness to new ideas, dedication to the art form, and consistent one-on-one relationship with a competent voice teacher, will help in building a beautiful, expressive, and well-balanced singing voice, a voice truly reflective of one's artistic goal.

I often refer to classical singing as the "Bentley" or "Rolls-Royce" of singing because it takes more time, practice, and dedication than any other vocal style to truly perfect. Similar to these luxury cars, *bel canto*'s attention to detail and critical evaluation is essential. That's why it takes so much commitment by the singer to perform classical repertoire, the repertoire I personally find most vocally rewarding. So, although I enjoy singing other styles of music, I prefer driving a Bentley.

WHY STUDY VOICE?

Consider asking yourself the following questions:

1. Why do I want to learn how to sing well?
2. When did I realize I loved singing enough to seriously pursue solo vocal study?
3. What are my singing intentions and goals (short, intermediate, and long term)?

Only by knowing your "why" will you be motivated to practice and improve. Students tell me they start taking lessons because "People say I'm good," "I want to be just like so-and-so," "I love music!" or "It makes me happy and brings happiness to people." All of these are great answers, but the student's motivation and dedication to singing and discipline regarding practicing and intensive vocal study need to be strong enough to keep on the road to real progress. Having good intentions or wishful thinking, having "natural" instincts, a unique sound, and/or a great appearance onstage will only get the student so far. They need to take voice lessons from a seasoned voice teacher and maintain a good practice ethic to avoid developing bad vocal habits and causing physical harm to the vocal folds. In the following chapters I set out to augment the voice student's study by offering important techniques needed to build on their potential while maintaining their motivation and instilling a disciplined practice routine. It is my hope to help the serious voice student find the solid foundation needed for a more fulfilling, healthy, and long-lasting vocal life.

WHAT IS AND ISN'T IN THIS BOOK

The techniques and exercises I'll be sharing in the following pages are the by-product of the experiences and knowledge I've accumulated from masterclasses, colleagues, voice teachers, students, and performances throughout my training and career. I also draw on papers I've written on voice production, pedagogical articles, books, and professional music databases.

This book does not focus on phonetics, pronunciation, languages, or repertoire, but I do include a list of suggested online sources for some of these topics in Appendix II. Neither does this book delve into critical aspects of creating the well-rounded vocal musician, such as keyboard training, music theory, acting skills, the study of music history, literature, and other art forms.

The first part of this book contains chapters on the Mind Connection, Resonance Connection, Breath Connection, Language Connection, and Body Connection, which include examples and technical exercises and fixes for developing each area. Chapter Six deals with choosing a teacher, a guide to practicing, and more vocal fixes, followed by Appendix I, which deals with vocal faults and disorders. In Appendix II you'll find lists of online resources on vocal health and business, musical theater, contemporary commercial music (CCM), magazines/journals/organizations, and Facebook singer's groups and communities. This book is interspersed throughout with inspirational sayings from the classic book *Vocal Wisdom: Maxims of Giovanni Battista Lamperti* (1931), by the nineteenth-century master teacher Lamperti (1839–1910), and posthumously published by his student William E. Brown. I hope they bring you the same inspiration they have brought me.

Diagrams, images, videos, audio recordings, and other material related to the book are found in the associated website, beautifulsinging.org.

With dedication and true passion, you can aspire to do great things with your voice. Remember, there are no shortcuts to any artistic craft, only pathways that require dedication, perseverance, discipline, respect for the art, and a passion for beauty and excellence. Enjoy your journey into making this world a more beautiful place through singing.

MY VOCAL JOURNEY

I come from a musical family, particularly on my father's side. All the Felix relations were Welsh, and Wales is famous as the "Land of Song," especially for its male choirs. My paternal grandparents were well known in their South Dakota county for singing duets for more than three hundred weddings and funerals over the years, often with my grandma accompanying on the piano. She also played for two services every Sunday at their Congregational church, a white country church set in a field out on the Dakota plains. My entire family loved music, but it was my mom who first encouraged me to start studying piano when she noticed that I could hear a song play on the radio and then go plunk it out on the piano. I enjoyed it at first, but over the next few years I wanted to quit lessons many times. Then I began to like being able to play and we didn't have any more arguments about practicing. Later in this book I tell the story of my first piano recital and dealing with stage fright.

It was also at the age of six that I got hooked on singing. My older brothers were in the local 4-H Club, and the members wanted to do a piece from the musical *The Music Man* for the state talent contest. They needed a young boy to sing the big solo Ron Howard had sung in the movie. The show's director came to our house, and I guess he liked my audition because the next thing I knew I was onstage in front of hundreds of people pulling a little red wagon singing, "Oh, the Wells Fargo wagon is a coming down the street / Oh please let it be for me!" I loved every minute of it!

I grew up playing in the church bell choir and singing in the church choir, sometimes performing solos. When I reached junior high I began playing saxophone and got serious about singing after hearing a bass singer during a school assembly. It was my sophomore year in high school. Every Friday afternoon our school would have a one-hour student assembly where all its students would meet in the school's theater and watch a movie or listen to a guest speaker or musical artist. One week they presented this amazing bass singer who, with a fine piano accompanist, performed a recital of songs from *Don Quixote*, *South Pacific*, and other classic musicals. Since my voice had changed from soprano to bass the previous year, I was mesmerized and wanted to sing "just like that." After hearing such an amazing voice, I finally realized that I simply loved singing/music—I loved how it made me feel and made other people feel, and I eventually began to believe in myself. I found I had the desire to be a professional singer and artist, so I listened to as many famous singers as possible, often trying to imitate how they approached the music and produced the beautiful sound they were making. I eventually began to imagine what it would be like to perform with great singers in grand venues myself. So began my path to vocal artistry.

High school was a blur of musical activity—I recently looked at the diary I kept from tenth through twelfth grade and saw that I was rehearsing, practicing, and performing at least six hours a day, which included chamber and concert choir, jazz and concert band, voice contests, piano recitals, and all the musicals. I had excellent choir and band directors who took time to answer my questions and give me the occasional individual lesson. Along with my piano teacher, they were all active performers in their fields and wonderful role models for young musicians who wanted to pursue music as a profession. I'll never forget that they gave me my first classical, jazz, and opera records including Rachmaninoff's *2nd Piano Concerto*, Stan Getz's *10,000 Miles High*, and George London's *Of Gods and Demons*. Years later, when I was old enough to realize how generous that was, I was honored that they had cared enough to foster my love of music. High school was a great experience, but little did I know that I was to take twelve more years of schooling to become a professional classical singer.

My love of piano, saxophone, and voice made it tough to choose a college major, but I finally settled on a bachelor of fine arts in theater and voice. While at the University of Kansas, I drove my Honda CB 350 motorcycle all over Lawrence, even in the winter, and I was right in the middle of rehearsals as Figaro in the *Marriage of Figaro* when I had an accident. That night in February, I was driving home when a drunk driver who was going 60 in a 30 mph zone rear-ended me, sending me flying like a cannonball a full sixty feet. Needless to say, I should have been wearing a helmet, but luckily (or not) I came down on my left leg, cutting off the main artery at the knee and sending me to the hospital to get it grafted back together and recover for three weeks. It was a traumatic event that had implications on my career for the rest of my life.

My first opera experiences after university were in the chorus of Minnesota Opera and as an apprentice at Des Moines Opera and Opera Orlando. After moving to New York with my wife, soprano Antonia Felix, I sang with regional and national companies and festivals such as L'Opera Français de New York, American Chamber Opera, Ash-Lawn Highland Opera Festival, and Carmel Bach Festival. My first voice teacher in New York was Armen Boyajian, teacher to my idol, bass Samuel Ramey, and about five years after moving to the city I began teaching lessons out of our apartment. Like most singers, Antonia and I were making a living with "day jobs," in my case as a waiter at a restaurant at Lincoln Center and for Antonia as a copywriter at a publishing house. We both held church jobs as well, which we enjoyed very much. But my favorite job was teaching, which was one reason I wanted to continue my training at a conservatory.

Earning a master's degree at the Manhattan School of Music (MSM) gave me in-depth instruction in diction, languages, repertoire, movement, and both vocal and piano technique, and also offered some wonderful performing opportunities. Antonia and I will never forget how exciting it was to celebrate New Year's Eve 1999 with the MSM orchestra, chorus, and solo quartet, in which I was the baritone, performing Beethoven's Ninth Symphony at the Cathedral of St. John the Divine. What a way to celebrate ushering in the new millennium—and what a relief for everyone when the much-hyped techno meltdown they called Y2K never materialized. My goal of expanding my performing and teaching opportunities with the degree from MSM bore fruit not long afterward when I was hired to join the music faculty at Texas A&M University–Kingsville. I loved everything about the position, from the wonderful students to the new challenge of directing opera.

That first teaching position motivated me to return to graduate school for a doctorate at the University of Kansas, where I had earned my bachelor of fine arts degree. I chose KU partly because I would be able to study with my former voice teacher, John Stephens, and two of the highlights of those three years were performing the lead in Verdi's *Falstaff* and presenting my doctoral project, a lecture recital of my own art song compositions. Following KU, I joined the music faculty at nearby Emporia State University and launched Kansas Concert Opera, which performed in-state as well as in Kansas City, Missouri. The responsibilities of running a small arts organization like KCO ran the gamut from auditioning singers to designing newspaper ads and creating fundraising events. Fundraising—never ending, absolutely necessary, and really tough when a recession hits. After a few years in Emporia, Antonia and I decided to return to Minnesota to be closer to family and reengage with the arts community that had been a big part of our formative years. In Minneapolis I launched Minnesota Concert Opera (more fundraising!), where one season included a rare performance of "The Mini-Ring," a one-evening version of Wagner's four-opera *Der Ring des Nibelungen*. The production, cast with Jay Hunter Morris and other stars and made possible in collaboration with the Richard Wagner Society of the Upper Midwest, drew Wagner fans from all over the country and made the millions of production details entirely worth it. Since Minnesota Concert Opera produced its last work in 2015, I have continued teaching, conducting masterclasses, composing, and writing this book. The talented local singers and dedicated teachers I've met since my return to Minnesota are a testament to this region's strong vocal legacy. Even though there is probably more of a Scandinavian influence on the choral scene here than the Welsh one of my background, singing is in the heart of this place. After all, Minnesota is famous as the land of 10,000 lakes *and* the land of 10,000 choirs.

Whether you want to be a better choral singer or are pursuing a career in opera or musical theater, I have written this book for you. Every passion for developing the voice deserves a clear path toward understanding how the mind and body come together to create . . . beautiful singing.

ONE

The Mind-Body Connection

"'Know thyself' applies to singers more than to other professions, because to sing well, body, soul and mind are tuned together to do it." —LAMPERTI

"Dr. Felix, have you heard of Thomas Quasthoff?" Jim had just burst into my voice studio, breathless from trying to be on time for his lesson, and he seemed really excited. "I heard this guy on the radio driving over and I just had to keep listening until he was done. Sorry, am I late?" I waited for him to take off his jacket, catch his breath, and start the recording app on his cell phone. I assured him he was right on time and told him that Thomas Quasthoff was one of my favorite singers and one of the finest bass-baritones ever. Although he was most famous for his German lieder and oratorio work, he had actually mastered a lot of different styles. "You should hear him sing jazz," I said. "Man, can that cat scat!" I pulled out my smartphone and showed him a YouTube video of Quasthoff singing in a jazz club. Jim was completely blown away.

"I didn't know you could sing like that if you were a 'serious' singer," he said. We then began talking about Quasthoff's vocal resonance and large, round timbre, and how he was able to sing a variety of vocal styles with the use of the right acoustical space. By the end of the lesson we had worked out a number of new approaches. Jim left the lesson excited and ready to go home to practice what we'd just worked on.

For the last twenty-five years I've enjoyed teaching voice lessons to all types of students, beginner to advanced, and have taught vocal pedagogy at the university level for ten of those years. After a few weeks working with beginning voice students and seeing that they're improving and connecting to their support, I like to play them video and audio recordings of great singers in their voice category singing both classical and/or musical theater pieces. We then talk about how the performer breathes, his or her facial movements, their stage presence, and vocal technique. When we finish the analysis, I ask the student what they think about the performer's level of singing and musicianship. They usually react in one of two ways: "I want to be that good!" or "I'll never be that good." Along with having a good ear for pitch and natural musical abilities, it's the mindset of the student that really tells me if they're going to improve significantly and rise to a certain level of proficiency. Are they excited about the challenge of learning and do they love singing enough to do the work necessary to achieve their goal, or have they already decided their limits and approach their studies from a sense of lack?

That sense of lack may be in response to negative past experiences. Did their parents encourage their musical ambitions? Have they been positively reinforced by compliments when they sing? Did their brother or sister tease them when they sang, or were they born into a family that thought music was frivolous? When you're growing up, these things matter.

For example, I felt the sting of an early musical experience for years. I was six years old when I performed in my first piano recital at our local Presbyterian church. There were two pianos in front of the room and a nice-sized crowd of parents and friends in the audience. A number of students had played their pieces and I thought it was my turn to perform, so I went up to the piano on the left and began playing my piece. Well, as it turned out, it was actually another student's turn, and that little boy had gotten up at the same time and started playing the piano on the right. Surprised and embarrassed, I slinked back to my seat and sat down to wait my turn. When it was my time I reluctantly walked up to the stage and sat down at the piano. I was a bit flustered already, so when I started playing, I messed up and had to start over. My mother was in the front row watching all of this, and when I made the mistake, I heard her make a loud "tsk." Needless to say, I completely fell apart and did not do well for the rest of the piece. After this experience at my first recital I had serious *stage fright* for years.

This kind of experience has stopped many people from continuing their music studies. However, because I had a supportive and musical family (my mom's early critical moment aside), from a young age I knew music was going to be a big part of my life.

"Unity is maintained by linked action of all parts.
Over-action of one member endangers cooperation.
No-action of any part breaks a link and disrupts
co-ordination." —LAMPERTI

UNITY

The art of singing casts a large net when it comes to the elements needed to achieve a balanced and beautiful voice. Breath, resonance, posture, positioning, strength, and endurance are essential physical attributes, but spiritual and mental aspects are also needed to fully encompass the artistry known as singing. Without the cooperation between all of these aspects, the singer comes up short in creating a unified singing voice.

"Broaden your knowledge of literature, painting, etc. . . . This increases your 'desire' for beauty from which springs the instinct to sing." —LAMPERTI

ARTISTRY

The achievement of artistry is the optimal goal for any serious singer. In fact, a singer can only be called an artist if he or she has developed their skill and imagination to create beautiful experiences. Artistry is a matter of acting, feeling, and thinking at the highest level. Of course, when I first started working on my voice I had no idea what was involved in reaching the highest level of singing development. Achieving this level is elusive to many beginning singers because it can only be achieved through time and patience, an attribute most of us are lacking. Levels of development helpful in achieving artistry include:

- Development of all the technical skills necessary for communicating the art of singing (a high level of musicality), with the final intent being to no longer concentrate on those technical skills when performing.
- Learning to distinguish between the normal and extraordinary, an essential step toward creativity and sophisticated thought.
- Dissemination of stylistic and musicological information.
- The study of languages.

- The ability to re-create artistry for oneself through listening and imitation.

Most of these points, and the techniques essential to develop the voice, will be covered later in this book. But what about the initial spark? The need to sing no matter what? To be as good as you can be, no matter what? This is a little something called "desire."

"It is through our desires, our sensations, our perceptions, that we gain control of our activities in body and mind. This is especially true in singing." —LAMPERTI

DESIRE

Desire is the first step in attaining anything you want in life. It's the catalyst that forms all things seen in the imagination. If that desire is to be the best singer you can be, you have most likely had a good teacher or a singer role model whom you wanted to emulate, or who has encouraged you at an early stage of your vocal development. Maybe you had some great singing experience in school or a summer voice program. Whatever it was, you now consider singing a major part of your life and want to make the most of it. By taking lessons and practicing you are doing the physical work needed to develop your voice, and now you must seriously consider how to develop the mental and spiritual aspects of singing. Through your desire you can now imagine yourself as a great singer.

MOTIVATION

Desire and motivation are similar in many ways. So, what is the motivation behind being a singer? Does the desire or need to express oneself artistically define success for you? Or is it the desire to have wealth or attain fame? In either case it's the optimistic voice student who is motivated by an expectation of success. This optimistic expectation not only directs and energizes the student's studies in order to reach higher goals, but also helps them enjoy the journey that it takes to get there. This passion for singing is an element needed for success and is not found in the unmotivated or pessimistic student. Even though the pessimist may find the learning process interesting and have a technically beautiful voice and the ability to attain great heights in their singing endeavors, if they don't follow their passion, they will not achieve true success. To be truly happy and satisfied the motivation for the successful singer comes more from the heart than the brain. How else can the singer be emotionally successful in connecting with the music?

In a broad sense of the word, motivation could be called anything from within that directs decision making and the actions to be taken. So, where does the motivation to be a singer come from? This is a subject of much debate. As for myself, I believe there is an inherent need to create and to express oneself. One could also make the point that expressing oneself vocally, without the use of a musical instrument, is the most natural way to do that. Whether the student chooses singing as a way of expression is determined at a very young age. Positive feedback from parents, influential adults, and friends may have a great deal to do with it. The child may be musically inclined with a great ear to imitate, a good ear for pitch, and the appropriate concentration level for the study of music. If this musical ability is encouraged and reinforced, the student may find that their voice is their preferred medium in which to express that music. I know the positive feedback I received from congregation members hearing me sing solos in church at an early age was a major influence in my choosing the singing path. Later, my success at singing competitions and performances further supported this decision.

Although I think the core motivation for singing is the love of music, if the student is taught by a competent and encouraging voice teacher there will be even more motivation by the student to express that love of music. I was lucky. I had a choir director and band teacher in high school who were also great performers in their own right. Watching my teachers perform professionally strongly encouraged me to get into the business. For example, my choir director might sing the bass soloist part for the regional *Messiah* oratorio performance, or my band teacher would have me run the lighting while he played trap set in his professional jazz trio. A teacher's passion for teaching, their joy of performing, their instilling the joy of practice, and an ability to stretch and push the student toward excellence are great motivating factors in shaping an artist who is curious, driven, and self-motivated.

"To know the result before we act is the 'golden rule' of singing."
—L*amperti*

MENTAL IMAGERY

The student can only sing as well as they "think" they can sing. Therefore, there has to be some kind of reference to what great singing sounds like. If the student has no "best singers" as references to imitate or idolize, they are more likely to settle for less in their own singing efforts. A good teacher should have many audio and video recommendations of great singers for their students to peruse, along with their own ability to demonstrate all aspects of fine singing to their student. Also, the student who sings in a chorus should take that opportunity to observe how the guest soloists breathe, their posture, and their intent when they sing. By observing how excellent performers approach their music, the student can receive invaluable lessons on how to interpret their music correctly. This will then give the student an idea of what does and doesn't work in their own voice. This forms the mental imagery needed to express the quality of one's own voice. As Fields (1972) wrote:

> *Mental imagery provides the very plan and purpose of vocal expression. The formation of the sounds of the voice and their adequate projection are direct outpicturings of these underlying concepts, and vocal expression is therefore imagery. . . . Basically, it is the MIND that sings, not the voice. You can say or sing only what you think. Therefore, you can sing only as beautiful a tone as you can think, since your voice always follows your thoughts. . . . Hence, we must learn to sing in thought, for the tone is embedded in the idea that produces it.*

If you're confident in your vocal technique and your ability to interpret the correct notes and rhythms, and you've done your research listening to the great singers, it should not be a hard task for the mind to imagine a beautiful tone quality and develop a positive *vocal image*.

Mental imagery is also a wholistic (subjective) teaching approach that deals with simile and metaphor. Although the voice teacher's emphasis should always be to help the student find their own natural singing voice, instructing the student to sing "as if" or "like" someone can elicit a positive vocal response, often resulting in the use of imitation.

"Singing depends on the sense of hearing. The physical ear perceives and knows how pure tone sounds in voices. . . . The mental ear 'visions' little by little how to produce it. Singing is instinctive. Its control is subconscious." —LAMPERTI

IMITATION

A wonderful example of imitation happened when I was teaching voice to a class of instrumental majors at a university in Texas. The students were taking turns singing a piece they all had to learn and were told to incorporate a number of voice techniques they had studied so they could achieve the best sound possible. When it was a clarinet major's turn to sing, I stopped him immediately because we could hardly hear him. I told him to really "mean it" when he attacked the phrase. All of a sudden, this meek young man, who had barely been audible on any song that semester, let out an amazing operatic voice that completely blew the class and me away. When he'd finished the song, the class went wild! We couldn't believe that that much resonance, and that kind of sound quality, had come out of that quiet undergrad. When the class calmed down a little, I asked the young man what he had done to produce such a resonant sound. He told us, "I just imagined that I was an opera singer." We all remarked how wonderful it sounded and that he should always imagine that. Unfortunately, he felt that the sound was so foreign to him that he didn't feel comfortable enough to continue singing that way. He thought all of his friends would think he was strange, so he was too embarrassed to ever sing like that again in class.

Imitation and a "good ear" are key elements to becoming a great singer. That's why it's so important for the serious voice student to always be listening to recordings and to attend live performances of professional singers. Because, as the earlier quote points out, "you can sing only as beautiful a tone as you can think."

"The singing voice is a 'castle in the air.' Imagination is its architect. Nerves carry out the plans. Muscles are the laborers. The soul inhabits it." —LAMPERTI

IMAGINATION

A good imagination is essential for any great artist, especially the performing singer. Although being musically well prepared and having a quality sleep the night before can go a long way toward a successful performance, experiencing the event in the imagination before it happens can also have positive effects.

A major aspect of pre-performance preparation includes *positive imagery* and the ability to visualize what it's like to have just had a successful performance.

> *Exercise: Find a comfortable seat, sit down, and close your eyes. Imagine the sensations of sweat on your forehead, the warmth of the lights, the accompanist's or conductor's eyes as you communicate with each other. Allow yourself to experience the feeling of a successful performance before the performance has actually taken place. The relief and joy you feel are real and you're elated at the successful outcome. You hear the applause of the crowd during your third encore, you see people's reaction, hear their praise, and feel the touch of a person enthusiastically shaking your hand in the reception that follows.*

Visualization can also be helpful in reducing stage fright and increasing confidence. In the same way an athlete prepares for a performance, "visualizing successful performance has been found to increase confidence and will also help players [singers] manage their nerves. In this case, pictures are more powerful than words – picturing yourself doing well has been found to be more effective at enhancing mood and reducing anxiety than telling yourself that you will do well" (InnerDrive, 2019).

By using your imagination this way, you influence the outcome. It takes discipline, but this technique can be effective in all aspects of your life, especially goal making.

GETTING THE HEAD OUT OF THE WAY

I've always said that singers are some of the smartest people I know, but they think way too much! I find that the extremely analytical student has the most trouble getting the head out of the way and loosening up, always blaming themselves or trying too hard, and those who don't worry so much have the most fun, are freer onstage and sing with less tension.

Everyone is wired differently and is a creation of their personal and social histories. But it's also a *left/right brain* thing. While the left hemisphere is more analytical, logical, orderly, practical, and factual, the right hemisphere of the brain is more intuitive, spontaneous, creative, and visual (uses imagery). If you were encouraged to embrace your intuition and imagination when growing up, you may find it easier to explore your music in a more *wholistic* or open-minded manner (right side) rather than in a linear fashion (left side). Our educational system, for the most part, does not encourage use of the intuitive right-brain as much as the logical left-brain, so it is sometimes difficult for the two hemispheres to communicate with each other. This inability to integrate may affect the singer's mental focus and conception of themselves and how well they judge their own ability to sing well.

"When heart and head unite, self-knowledge results."
—LAMPERTI

MENTAL FOCUS

Singers can fall into two camps when it comes to their psychological approach to the art. The intellectual approach deals with the mechanical use of established vocal technique. The intellectual struggle and the act of "trying" that can be said to be ego-driven primarily deal with the "process" rather than the "product" of singing. By concentrating more on the technique than on interpretation there is a chance that the singer may be missing out on the main purpose one sings in the first place: that of expressing him or herself.

With an intuitive, or truthful focus, the singer puts ego in its proper place and creates art that transcends "trying" by performing from the place where creativity, musicality, personality, interpretation, and true expression lie. A sense of intimacy is conveyed to the audience as a result of the singer's willingness to share their vulnerability.

Singers who connect truthfulness with a good sense of pitch are sometimes said to have "talent." Often, talented singers feel that intuitive focus is enough to be a good singer. But the great singer knows that the knowledge found in the intellectual focus is just as important and has to be integrated with the intuitive in order to produce a well-rounded singer.

"You can sing when in the roots of your being you know you can." —LAMPERTI

CONCEPTION

How do you perceive yourself? Do you think you're a good singer? How do you perceive the art form you're pursuing? Is it worthy of your time and effort? Is it something you're proud of working on? Why are you in music? If you don't know these answers, you have some soul searching to do.

If you're not sure why you're doing it, but just know how great you feel when you are, that's half the battle. What you need now is some more inspiration. Go to more concerts, watch all those enlightening masterclasses available on the internet, steep yourself completely in your craft and the people associated with it. Do a summer program, do more auditioning, set up a recital. Have something to work for. Dress the part. Just like in any relationship, you have to give it your undivided attention to make it work. If you make the decision to give it your all, then truly give it your all, because you can't be your best without the practice time needed. You owe it to the art, and yourself, not to do it halfway.

But maybe you think you're already good enough. Maybe you have the illusion that you're better than most singers and you don't have to work that hard or listen to your teacher so much. Well, there are singers who think that way, no matter how unfounded their conclusion.

"When knowledge of singing is truly realized and vital, it carries the necessary action with it." —LAMPERTI

SELF-PERCEPTION

What is happening when a person thinks they sing better than they really do? They might be exhibiting what Nico Van Yperen and Bram Buunk (1991) defined as *illusory superiority*, a cognitive bias that happens when a person overestimates their qualities and abilities. Also known as the *Dunning-Kruger Effect*, named after psychologists David Dunning and Justin Kruger (2000), who explain that "the miscalibration of the incompetent stems from an error about the self, whereas the miscalibration of the highly competent stems from an error about others."

People from any walk of life can, in many other occupations, sometimes exhibit a neurological disorder caused by physiological damage to the parietal lobe of the right hemisphere of the brain, which causes a deficit of their own self-awareness (otherwise known as *anosognosia*). In *Self-insight: Roadblocks and Detours on the Path to Knowing Thyself* (2005), Dunning describes the Dunning-Kruger Effect as "the anosognosia of everyday life," referring to a condition that hinders self-reflection. People with anosognosia cannot perceive their condition, so they can't address it. Dunning (2005) writes, "If you're incompetent, you can't know you're incompetent. . . . The skills you need to produce a right answer are exactly the skills you need to recognize what a right answer is."

Another type of self-delusion similar to the Dunning–Kruger Effect would be the *Lake Wobegon Effect*, where one overestimates one's abilities and considers oneself "above average," on a scale from grandiose delusions to hubris and optimism bias. While the Dunning-Kruger Effect highlights the fact that we are vulnerable to severely inaccurate perceptions of ourselves, two other conditions are more closely aligned to the singing profession, narcissism and the four stages of competence.

Narcissism

According to the *Diagnostic and Statistical Manual of Mental Disorders* (5th edition: DSM-5, 2013), narcissistic personality disorder (NPD) is defined as a "pervasive pattern of grandiosity, need for admiration, and a lack of empathy." Although people with NPD often suffer from a lack of self-esteem, self-confidence, and self-worth, they often put on the air of confidence to appear very secure. The term comes from Greek mythology—Narcissus was a handsome young man who rejected the advances of a young woman named Echo. As punishment for rejecting her, the gods made him fall in love with himself by looking at his reflection in a pool of water until he eventually turned into a flower.

I have certainly run across some self-absorbed singers in my career, but at the same time I have always known that it takes a healthy ego and sense of self-worth to get somewhere in the competitive world of professional music. Having an adequate amount of these attributes has kept me from being devastated by criticism (though it always hurt a bit), has given me the nerve to go back to the next auditions to "try, try again," and has helped me stay focused on my goals. I knew that my self-worth was a result of hard work and years of practice. I knew that I could compete with other trained singers because of the correct vocal technique ingrained in me by knowledgeable teachers. I wasn't deluding myself. I didn't walk into the audition with the illusion that I was good enough; I felt I had a right to be there.

The spread of narcissism in the form of an exaggerated sense of competence and entitlement that we have seen in voice students in recent generations began, believe it or not, with the invention of the birth control pill in the early 1960s. Women could now make an important choice between career, family, or both. Couples could choose to have smaller families, and their children received much more attention than they would have had in a family of four or five siblings. Because more money was available, these children were often given anything they wanted and usually didn't have to share with siblings. They were told by their parents that they were very special, that they could excel at anything they did and be anything they wanted to be. They were told that the most important thing was to be themselves and to love themselves first before anything else. Sounds great. So, what went wrong?

In her book *The Narcissism Epidemic: Living in the Age of Entitlement* (2009), Dr. Jean Twenge refers to this new generation as "Generation Me," brought up with yearly school graduations, trophies for just doing one's best, and grades (or scores) often higher than they deserve. According to Twenge, school grade inflation had reached a record high among American college freshmen in 2004 with 48 percent of them reporting that they received an "A" average in their senior year of high school. Compare this to 1968, when only 18 percent of college freshman reported earning an A average in their last high school year. This all occurred while SAT scores decreased. Of course, a lot of teachers don't want to disappoint their students and upset their parents, so they find it easier to give them that "A" or superior rating in school music competitions. It's just too much work to explain a lower grade, and besides, those high scores reflect well on the school and help the teacher's chance for a raise or promotion in their next evaluation. The problem is that this not only fosters mediocrity in the schools, but also encourages the student, when faced with a teacher who insists on them studying or practicing, to cheat or lie so they can keep their grades at a level they feel they deserve. And since the students have been told their entire life that they are perfect just the way they are, why would they believe a teacher who tells them they're not? According to Peter Sacks (2008), author of *Generation X Goes to College: An Eye-opening Account of Teaching in Postmodern America,* these students have an extraordinarily thin skin and noted that the students who had such high self-esteem became rude, unfriendly, and uncooperative when criticized. Not good! Especially if they intend to be our future voice teachers and choir directors.

There is no place for an unhealthy amount of narcissism in a voice studio or classroom. Voice teachers need to know what to look for, then identify and rectify any negative attitudes early. They need to start or continue to expect more from their students by stretching them artistically and intellectually. Then, by showing them the encouragement, support, and respect they genuinely earn, we can stop this inclination toward mediocrity. Our students deserve it.

THE FOUR STAGES OF COMPETENCE

The technique of being consciously aware of one's singing abilities increases in stages, and only after years of practice and experience. Noel Burch's four stages for learning any new skill, developed in the 1970s (Gordon Training International, 2016), may help the singer realize where they are in their vocal development. What stage do you think you are?

Unconscious Incompetence: This student has no idea how they sound or whether they have the talent or ability to pursue a singing career. Although ignorance can be bliss, the student likes music and is interested in singing. It would be helpful for them to know if there is any real voice there, however.

Conscious Incompetence: The student knows a little about music and has probably sung occasionally in school or church choir. They enjoy singing and have learned a few techniques, but everything is still mostly unfamiliar. Not the most fun level to be on.

Conscious Competence: The student has been singing two or three years and has mastered a host of new skills. Things have really improved and they've received positive feedback about their voice. The problem is, they still need to concentrate to keep a consistent and effective technique working.

Unconscious Competence: This is the level we all strive for. Vocal technique is now habitual and the singer is now free to express themselves with the musicality one learns to expect in a well-trained voice. Singing is fun and easy, and confidence is high.

By first learning the craft of singing, and by learning vocal technique so well that it's automatic, the singer arrives at a musicality level of "unconscious competence." But the singer now must choose which kind of focus they will use. And it's not always the easiest decision to make. One has to decide whether to play it safe intellectually or to trust the training to be there when needed, allowing the training to be a vehicle for intuitive focus.

"Your conscious act must result from your instinctive 'urge.'"
—*LAMPERTI*

BEING PRESENT IN THE MOMENT

Being present in the moment is much easier said than done. It requires *mindfulness* (defined by the American Psychological Association [2012] as: "a moment-to-moment awareness of one's experience without judgment"). Making sure that in our daily practice we are working with correct tempos and rhythms, with conscious reflection on the feelings written into the lyrics, and using the correct breathing technique, are but a few examples of this focused meditation which is *mindfulness*. Matthew Giobbi, in his article "Mindfulness Through Music: An Introduction" (2020), explains:

> *Mindfulness can enhance our experience of being a musician. This is the application of mindful meditation towards the peak practice and performance of music. . . . Through instruction, daily meditative practice, and weekly discussions with a teacher, one can gain insight and initiate positive change in their practice and performance of music.*

If concentration does not come naturally, it should be practiced. That is, practiced with awareness in an impartial way. For example, before you start singing a phrase or vocalize, take the time to think about what you're doing, how much breath to take, how you're going to attack the first note. If you don't have a game plan when you practice, make one up and keep to it. We will cover more on how to practice in Chapter Six. Concentration while playing the piano or singing ensures optimal coordination between the brain and the muscles, just as it does in any sport. This concentration can also be solidified by the use of attitude and intent.

ATTITUDE/INTENT

Interpretation of the song's text is a matter of attitude and intent. Without these approaches, the singer shows no musical expression.

They are basically "phoning in" their performance, and the audience will not be moved emotionally. Attacking a phrase and expressing a word should all be done with intent; otherwise there will be a lack of energized breath behind it. Attitude is the catalyst for intent and can be achieved through empathy with the lyrics and development of acting skills (serious singers should always study acting). By using an emotion or attitude to activate the intent needed to energize the breath and interpret the text, the singer no longer relies on just singing the notes by rote.

"When the singer uses his intelligence and emotion on a 50-50 basis, he is an artist. His success is as great as his personality."
—LAMPERTI

PERSONALITY

When speaking, we are "sized up" by others through the *vocal image* we emit. When the voice is used in a convincing manner, like on the phone, the aural impression can be one of the most vital and controlling factors representing a speaker's vocal image. Strength, expressivity, intelligence, and emotion are all a reflection of personality best expressed through the speaking voice using correct diction, tone quality, and dynamics.

This is also true in the singing voice. Although earlier in their studies, singers are usually paying more attention to "how to sing," their main objective is to be expressive and musical (using intuitive focus) while finding meaning in the text—otherwise, what is the real purpose of singing?

Transferring one's personality into expressive singing can only be achieved when vocal technique is mastered first. Thus, personality makes a good singer a great singer. It's what makes the audience believe you when you're up there onstage. In musical theater, being a singer-actor means being able to sing in this style at the highest level as well as interpret the role as a fine stage actor. When performing opera and classical music, one must also be a singer-actor, performing with the resonance and beauty of a strong technique and relaying the intent behind the text as clearly and with as much expression as possible. These aspects will be covered to some extent in the "Empathy and Intent" and "Work It Like a Monologue" sections of Chapter Four.

FEELING, NOT LISTENING

Quit listening to yourself! Yes, I know, it's easier said than done. But feeling the vibration or ring (called *squillo*) in the facial *mask* (the facial area around the eyes and nose), created by years of practice developing optimal acoustics in the vocal tract (formant tuning), is much more important than listening to yourself. Besides, what the singer hears is often a poor representation of what kind of sound is actually being produced.

For example, say you've been practicing in a small practice room for a month. Your jury or recital is coming up and you think everything is sounding great. Then the day comes, and you walk out onstage of the recital or concert hall and start singing. What the—! All of a sudden you can't hear yourself. The resonance and acoustics you're used to, your voice's reflection off the practice room walls, is gone. So, what do you do to correct the sound your hearing? Do you push until you *can* hear yourself? Absolutely not! You remember what that resonant "buzz" in your head felt like in the practice room and you trust your technique.

Acoustics outside of the body are always going to be different, but the acoustics in your head, which you have developed over years of practice, will never fail you. Just be conscious of how the ring feels in the "mask" when it's happening. Remember and memorize that feeling, and then reenact it in all practice and performance situations.

WHICH PEDAGOGY APPROACH WORKS BEST FOR YOU?

There are two approaches to teaching and learning singing, *wholistic* and *mechanistic*. If you're a student who prefers an inspirational and intuitive approach to singing, you may want a teacher who tends to teach more wholistically. If you're a student who is scientifically or realistically minded, you may benefit the most from a voice teacher who works with a mechanistic style of teaching pedagogy. Although these pedagogies are quite different, in many ways a good voice teacher is well acquainted in the teaching of both approaches. Also, the student will benefit immensely in using a combination of these approaches in a more integrated, or *eclectic* style.

Mechanistic

The mechanistic approach works best for students who need to know exactly what muscles are being used and the anatomical settings it takes to sing well. It is a more "left brained" or analytical and logical approach and encourages the student to consciously create the voice they want. Demonstration and imitation are often used as tools, as well as applying a close connection to the way one speaks in producing the correct phonemes (see "Speech vs. Singing" in Chapter Four).

Wholistic

The wholistic approach seems to work the best with those "right-brained" individuals who, through encouraging the natural, subconscious, psychological, and inspirational tendencies in one's voice, also use mental imagery to exhibit the natural voice that has been latent. Wholistic teachers often use poetical figures of speech and simile-based instruction such as "as if" or "like" to elicit a response from the student, therefore emphasizing the use of metaphor and encouragement for the student to be their own person and define their own goals.

Since all of my students have varied degrees of mechanistic or wholistic ways of thought, I always have at least eight different ways of saying the same thing when explaining vocal technique to them. As you will find in this book, I explain vocal technique with an eclectic mixture of both approaches.

In the next chapter I'll explain the different aspects of resonance and acoustics that result from the use of a good mixture of eclectic vocal technique.

TWO

The Resonance Connection

"To anticipate the 'feel' of resonance (vowels) before singing, and to keep the sensation during pauses and after singing, is the lost art of the Golden Age of Song."
—LAMPERTI

THE FORMATION OF RESONANCE IN THE SINGING VOICE

The quality, or beauty, of a singing voice allows both the trained and untrained ear to enjoy and aesthetically connect with the performer. Resonance quality is one of the most important aspects in determining whether the singer producing the sound is well trained in the art of singing. But is tone quality or timbre really something the singer has developed after years of study and practice, or is it a natural phenomenon? Is quality of tone in a singing voice something programmed into the listener since childhood, or does the actual sound produced need to have certain essential physical attributes contributed to it?

This chapter helps explain the physical determinants of good resonance in the professional singer, how these "vocal signatures" are produced, and how these singers, as a result of years of study and practice, produce habitual coordination between different parts of the vocal tract.

For example, there is a misconception by many singers that they must pull the vowels back into the mouth to mix with the lowered larynx and raised soft palate to find the resonance they're looking for. This is often referred to as the optimum "sweet spot" where all the acoustic elements come together, or in Italian, the *bel canto* term *chiaroscuro* (light-dark).

However, this balance of light and dark is actually created in two areas of the vocal tract. Chiaro is created by placement and oscuro by resonant space, used in tandem (along with the correct breath support) to find the ideal acoustic position. These areas are:

1. Forward placement (imagine one inch in front of the mouth) controls the bright quality of sound (chiaro) through pure vowel placement, balanced air flow, and engaged lips.
2. Lowered larynx, raised soft palate, and correct placement of the tongue control the dark and resonant quality of sound (oscuro) by allowing access to a low breath and allowing more space for sound to resonate. How much space one needs depends on which style of singing they choose (Example: lots of space for classical, less space for musical theater and contemporary styles such as rock and pop).

The harmonics created by this balance between forward placement and lowered larynx/raised soft palate are called formants. In this chapter we'll cover all the aspects of resonance, starting with what Bloothooft and Plomp (1986) refer to as "a high-frequency peak in the vowel spectra . . . which was said to add 'ring' to the voice," called the singer's formant.

"Noise is a naked skeleton. Tone is fleshed in its own harmonics, and clothed in the overtones of surrounding space." —LAMPERTI

FORMANTS

Formants are frequencies energized by resonance cavities in the vocal tract also known as partials, overtones, or resonances. Once air has caused the vibrator (vocal folds) to phonate, the fundamental sound continues up the vocal tract, where the tone is enhanced by the two main resonating cavities, the throat and mouth (the laryngopharynx and the oropharynx). The throat is positioned above the vocal cords, where it acoustically enhances the fundamental "buzz" made by the vibrator. As Garyth Nair (1999) tells us:

> *The resonator of any musical instrument, including the voice, favors some harmonics while dampening others. In the human voice, this source is in the vocal folds, which vibrate (open and close) at rates anywhere from about 60 to 1,200 times per second in singing. The resonator, which selects certain harmonics for amplification, is the vocal tract—the partially enclosed air space between the vocal folds at one end and the openings at the lips and nostrils at the other. This complex resonator has a series of variable resonances, called formants.*

The hard and soft palate then control the length of the vocal tract's resonating cavities, producing a specific sound quality and different intensities of component harmonics. Once the resonated sound waves move into the mouth, adjustments and shapes made by the articulators (tongue, lips, teeth, and jaw) help to maintain the optimal length of the vocal tract and efficiency of the breath, and shape the vowels and consonants needed for speech and singing.

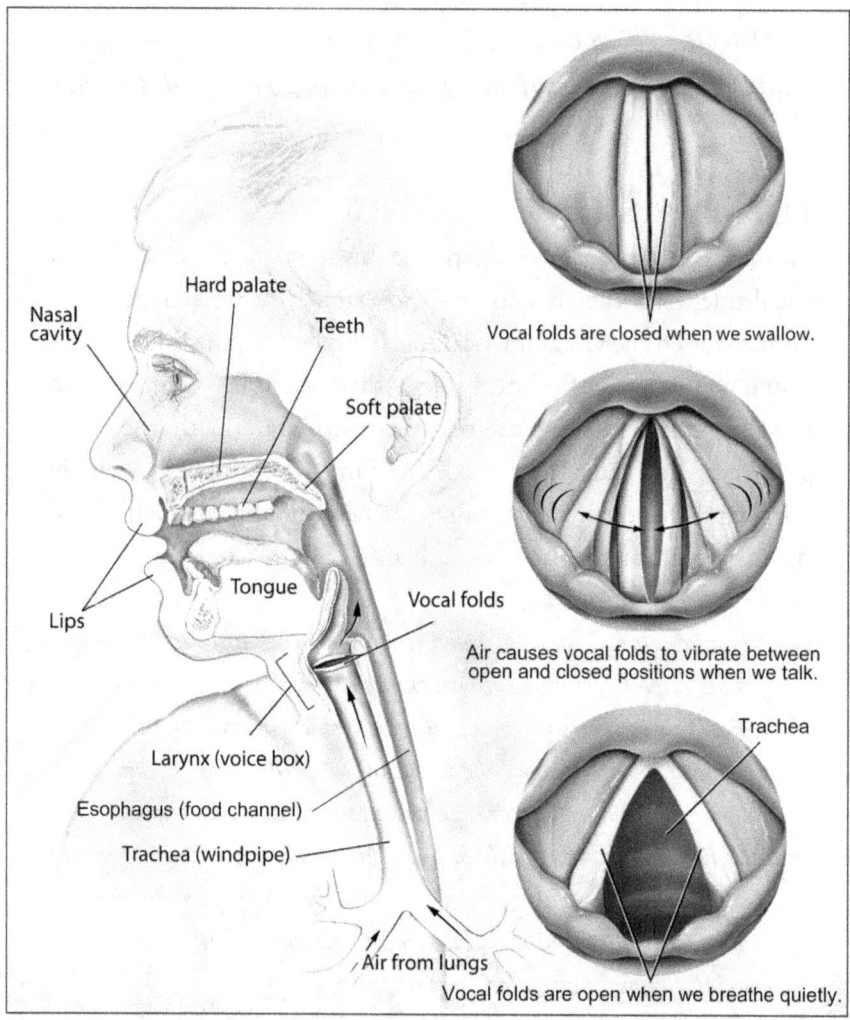

Figure 1. Anatomy of the Human Voice.

As early as 1879, Alexander Graham Bell said in the *American Journal of Otology* that all vowels have double resonances and help lay the foundation for the acoustical law of fixed formants in vocal sound.

There are two types of formants:

Separated: Created by open vowels (Example: "ah" or "oh"): this space in the vocal tract causes a distribution of energy between two widely spaced formants, causing ring and brilliance to the tone quality.

Clustered: Associated with closed vowels (Example: "ee" and "ih"), these two close-frequency bands help to tune and infuse the tone quality with depth and mellowness.

According to Barbara Doscher (1994), a formant may be defined as "a specific concentration of energy within the vocal sound wave." This sound wave is composed of many harmonic frequencies that are partials and overtones of the fundamental frequency. It is manipulated by the different articulators such as the tongue and lips to correspond with a sympathetic resonating space in the vocal tract, causing a concentration of tonal energy or "formant." Doscher (1994), quoting D. Ralph Appelman, further explains formants:

As the sound passes through the resonating cavities of the throat and mouth, the profile of the spectrum changes, since each cavity resonates to some of the tones in the spectrum more readily than to others and each adds its own characteristics to such tones. This reinforcement gives the partials greater energy at the point of cavity resonance. These points of greater energy are called formants.

Although speech and musical instruments contain a fundamental frequency, also called F0, and the two lower formants of F1 and F2, singers use five major formants. These include the two lower vowel formants of F1, produced by the throat or pharynx, and F2, which is produced in the mouth with lip and tongue movements and determines the vowel color. Also used by highly trained singers are F3, F4, and F5, which are called quality formants and make up an individual singer's timbre and personality. These top three are also called the singer's formants.

> *"The more evident the sensation of resonance in the cavities of head and mouth, the better the 'placement' of voice."*
> —LAMPERTI

THE SINGER'S FORMANT

When the singer reinforces the fundamental frequency with adequate vocal fold contact, correct vowel placement, and acoustical tuning techniques (i.e., formant tuning), as explained in this book, the upper three quality formants (F3, F4, F5) are used. These singer's formants amplify even the smallest person's voice, enabling it to be heard over an entire orchestra. The singer's formant, which has frequencies caused by a high-spectrum peak, occurs between around 2,500 Hz and 3,200 Hz (Ware, 1998).

Formant Tuning

Johan Sundberg (1987) explains the complicated subject of formant tuning as follows:

> *Tuning the formant frequencies is done by changing the shape of the vocal tract: the jaw, the tongue, the lip opening, the larynx, and the side walls of the pharynx. Adult females have shorter vocal tracts than adult males. Therefore, their formant frequencies are 15% higher on average than those of the adult male. Adjusting the shape of the vocal tract is the most common method for tuning the formant frequencies.*

- *The first formant is responsive to the jaw opening.*
- *The second formant responds to the tongue shape.*
- *The third formant is responsive to the position of the tip of the tongue and to the size of the cavity between the lower teeth and the tongue.*
- *The fourth and fifth formants are more difficult to control these means.*

Although vocal pedagogues Johan Sundberg and Berton Coffin (1980), along with acoustician Pierre Delattre, have developed an intricate system of adjusting acoustical resonances to achieve the best harmonic response available, singing teachers have not embraced this formant tuning technique wholeheartedly because there has not been a practical means of measuring the singing voice's formant frequencies. Application of this technique was left to the ear of the singing teacher.

There is now, however, a helpful aid to visually detect formant frequencies. VoceVista, the voice analysis software developed in the Groningen Voice Research Lab in the Netherlands in the 1990s, creates a real-time image of the voice's resonance spectrum on a computer screen. I provide a more detailed explanation how VoceVista works in Appendix I. After this product came on the market, I attended a workshop on the implementation of the software led by codeveloper Donald Gray Miller, Ph.D. (1943–2020), after which I developed and taught a course called "Voice Building Through Acoustic Feedback" at Emporia State University in Kansas. I have found VoceVista to be an important visual aid in formant tuning when used in conjunction with well-trained interpretive ears of a highly trained teacher.

> *"Although you may acquire a wide range of voice, you cannot modulate the sounds until the resonance of your tones becomes round and rich,* chiaroscuro." —LAMPERTI

Resonance

As I explained about formant tuning, to make the optimal sound quality and resonance, the classical singer must try to adjust a particular partial/overtone/harmonic to the formant frequency by first using the soft palate and larynx, and then the articulators (tongue, teeth and lips) to shape the resonating space. While each formant frequency is determined by the shape of the vocal tract (such as the raising or lowering of the soft palate and larynx), articulators are also used by singers almost instinctively to search for the position of best resonance for any given vowel or note. By shaping the resonating space in this way, the singer augments the overtone or partial and achieves optimum frequency.

When you sing, does your voice feel "stuck" or sound like you have a cloth lodged in your throat? Poor tongue placement and impure vowels are usually the problem. The singer needs to keep the tongue out of the way and use pure vowels in order to avoid a "damping" of the sound wave and achieve the maximum resonance. This damping effect happens when the size and shape of the vocal tract is inconsistent with what is required for good resonance. Remember, a beautiful pure tone is a result of good acoustical structure in the vocal tract. When you modify or pull the vowel back (Example: "uh" instead of "ah," "ih" instead of "ee"), this pulls up the back of the tongue, restricting airflow and damping the sound to create an effect similar to singing into a heavy curtain. This causes the singer to try to push through the obstruction and makes singing much more work than necessary. If it's work to sing, your vocal tract is not in an acoustically optimal position.

The opposite is true when vowel placement is pure and forward in the mouth. Along with a slight flaring of the lips ("oo" lips are explained later in this chapter), this creates the correct airflow and least resistance, making it much easier to sing. There are a number of misguided reasons the inexperienced singer may want to modify a vowel and cause damping:

1. A need to blend and not stick out in choir. This causes some singers to try to mix with the rest of the section by pulling back their lips (I call this "choir lips") and causes a damping effect. This eventually turns into a bad vocal habit.
2. Wanting to sound more mature or older. Pulling back the vowel puts the sound in the back of the mouth closer to the ears, thus making the singer think they sound louder and fuller than they actually do. Pulling back and distorting the vowel actually stops the sound from resonating and projecting the distance needed to be clearly heard by the audience.

When I was fourteen, my voice changed from soprano to bass and I had no idea how I was supposed to sound. I had been singing in children's church choirs since the second grade, but singing with this new voice was foreign to me. Later, in tenth grade, I began taking voice lessons with my high school choir director, who sang all the major bass roles in the area, so he instructed me in correct repertoire. He also encouraged me to listen to recordings of some of the great bass and baritone singers. Of course, I wanted to sound more like my teacher and the mature voices I listened to, so in impersonating the operatic "big boys" I later realized I had pulled back and modified the vowels (Example: distorting the "ee" to "ih" or "ah" to "uh"), placing the sound closer to my ears and creating a much louder sound in my head. "Pretty close," I thought. But the distortion of the vowel had actually created a false resonance and thrown my voice out of balance. The pulling back of the tongue had caused a damping of the sound wave and thrown the sound into the nasal cavities instead of allowing an open acoustical resonance to be formed in the throat and mouth. It was loud in my head, but it didn't carry very far. This vowel distortion also hindered my ability to increase my range, often made pitch go flat, distorted the text, and made me want to push.

This problem persisted to some degree in college and into my early professional years. I sometimes heard the comment, "I know you have more voice there!" from teachers and coaches, and bit by bit they helped me open my resonance. Later, with their help and personal self-evaluation while I was teaching voice, I discovered how to produce more point and brightness to the sound by coordinating airflow through the use of pure vowels, acoustical positioning (formant tuning), and diction. This, when mixed with a lowered larynx and lifted soft palate, created what I was looking for—an optimal rich resonance with the least resistance. In other words, a balanced sound (*chiaroscuro*).

Personally, I felt like I was producing less sound because the placement was now at my lips instead of back by my ears, but that sound actually carried much further and was acoustically much louder and resonant, creating the ring in the voice discussed earlier. And because I was no longer blocking the airflow with a distorted tongue and pulled-back lips, I actually increased my "in performance" upper range by a major third, while top notes during practice were a fifth above what I had been able to reach before.

The best part, however, was that singing was no longer a lot of work! Before I figured out the correct placement and balance it was always so difficult to sing, and I really didn't have as much fun. On any given day I would rate the difficulty by comparing it to moving through substances of varying thicknesses.

Mud or molasses. I hated singing on these days. It was so much work and I felt like I was always pushing. I later realized that the tongue and lips were entirely in the wrong position, usually as a result of poor vowels, or a need to hear myself.

Water. I was finding it easier to sing on these days. There was less resistance because of better acoustical positioning of articulators and less soft tissue damping. The sound was smaller to me but projected more to the audience.

Air. On these days there was no resistance. Vowels, lips, and tongue were in their optimal acoustical position. A "ringing" in the mask and a well-balanced airflow indicated better acoustical output and better breath control.

As explained in the sample above, the inability to find the right acoustic space in conjunction with the appropriate glottal pressure caused a damping effect, resulting in the shortening of the sound waveform, less sound, and a stuck feeling. If the vocal tract is not the appropriate shape and length to realize a completed waveform, it will lack the formants/partials/overtones needed for resonate sound. This can be remedied, however, with a good ear, correct acoustical positioning (i.e. formant tuning), and a supported breathing technique.

"Though vibration alters its pitch, it does not change its place (pharynx)." —LAMPERTI

VIBRATO'S EFFECT ON RESONANCE

A significant aspect of the quality and timbre of a singing voice is vibrato, or the sound variation no more than one semitone above and below the center frequency, which is repeated at a rate of five to six times a second. Found in practically all correctly formed classically sung tones, it is an indication of a relaxed throat and helps give the impression that the tone is centered on pitch. A smooth, even vibrato is usually an indication of a healthy, coordinated technique. However, an irregular vibrato usually means there is a battle going on between the breath, vocal cord vibration, and resonance.

Two of these irregularities are the tremolo and the wobble. The tremolo (or flutter) has a rapid vibrato rate of more than 7.5 oscillations per second and fluctuates wildly in intensity and pitch. The wobble, which is usually caused by muscle fatigue or old age, has a very low number of oscillations, less than 5.5 per second. Both of these conditions indicate that the muscles in the throat are out of balance. I will explain these conditions and how to remedy them later in Chapter Six.

"The feeling that your tone is free, borne on its own wings of energy, is one of the greatest delights of life—because you are its creator." —LAMPERTI

THE EFFECT OF VOLUME ON RESONANCE

A common mistake often made by beginning and intermediate voice students is the use of too much effort to project their voice. As John Stephens, my doctoral voice teacher at the University of Kansas, always said, "You don't make the tone; you release it." Trying to push a lot of air through the vocal tract only flattens and straightens the tone and puts unneeded pressure on the apparatus. The correct technique is quite the opposite. It is the resonance created by correct vowel placement and shaping of the space that creates the volume they are looking for. Sure, in loud passages more breath is going through the vocal cords, but the full, "hooked-up" sound of the singer's formant is what carries the voice over a full orchestra. As Johan Sundberg (1977) explained, "because it is generated by resonance effects alone, it calls for no extra vocal effort; the singer achieves audibility without having to generate extra air pressure."

> *"When your tone issues from the focus of vibration, you are singing."* —LAMPERTI

THE LARYNGEAL COLLAR

There is an auxiliary resonating space, which in 1949 William Vennard named the laryngeal collar, which lies directly above the vocal folds and is isolated from the articulators. This small space is formed by lowering the larynx enough so the pharyngeal sidewall tissues are stretched, which contributes to the widening of the lower pharynx. This seems to aid in the clustering of the third, fourth, and fifth formant in a medium position that produces the resonating effect known as the singer's formant, or the "2800" (referring to the frequency rate of 2800 to 3500 Hz). James McKinney (2005) quotes Sundberg as saying, "Since the singer's formant can be present in all sounds, it must be comparatively insensitive to vowel articulation . . . the laryngeal tube is the part of the vocal tract that varies the least with vowel articulation." Sundberg (1987) adds that three of the main conditions needed to generate the singer's formant are lowering of the larynx, widening of the laryngeal ventricle, and widening of the pyriform sinuses (the bottom part of the vocal tract surrounding the laryngeal tube).

Using a relaxed lowered jaw is important in lowering the larynx to access the laryngeal collar, along with raising the soft palate in order to develop a nice, open-throated, resonant sound. According to McKinney (2005):

> *There are several areas in or adjacent to the larynx that might resonate (the brilliance and ring of the singer's formant). . . . Among them are the collar of the larynx, the Ventricles of Morgani (the pockets between the true and false cords), the vallecula (the space between the tongue and the epiglottis), and the pyriform sinuses (between the collar of the larynx and the thyroid cartilage). Another more distant area is that between the faucial pillars and the back wall of the pharynx.*

THE FALSE VOCAL CORDS-VESTIBULAR FOLDS

The false vocal cords, positioned above both the true vocal cords and the laryngeal collar, is part of a group of constricting muscles used to close the air passageway when drinking or eating. They then open up when inhaling a breath. The false vocal cords can be a source of many problems for the classical singer and must be trained to stay open as much as possible through the vocal line. Unless the singer has learned how to keep the throat loose and open, the false cords will start to close as they ascend to the higher end of their range (making those upper notes tight), or when they allow emotion to take over.

The false vocal cords can be very effective in contemporary styles of singing. An example of this is the use of vocal fry (which we will discuss in the registers section later in this chapter) and glottal starts and stops in the vocal line. There are many effects and colorings used in rock, R&B, jazz, pop, and other styles where the false vocal cords can be engaged. Guttural sounds, grunts, growls, yelps, yodels, and cries are a few of those effects. However, except when appropriately and intently used to convey emotion and color the vocal timbre, the false cords can get in the way when it comes to having the unobstructed open throat used in classical singing. We will be discussing how to keep these cords as loose and open as possible later in the book.

"Only when the fullest acoustical resources of the instrument have been successfully exploited will the purest quality and fullest resonance be achieved." —REID (1950)

TIMBRE

Timbre is the characteristic sound that distinguishes a singer's (or instrumentalist's) sound quality, produced by using the adductory force of the vocal folds, vestibular folds, false vocal cords, and acoustical overtones in the throat and mouth. In other words, formant frequencies determine the personal timbre in the voice. Vibrato is also a contributing factor and a major contributor of changing timbre patterns (sonance) such as pitch and intensity. Finding different tones/colors/timbres in the voice is a by-product of acoustics and the singer's ability to adjust the space in the vocal tract (formant tuning). It is quite unique to each singer and actually gives other people the ability to identify you by sound alone.

Characteristics of tone/timbre in a balanced singing voice should include:

1. Both bright and dark tonal qualities (*chiaroscuro*). Warm and rich yet with a nice ring (*squillo*). These qualities are manipulated formant structures made by adjustments of the mouth opening while singing pure vowels.

2. A relaxed, even vibrato with an oscillation rate of between 5.5 and 7.5 oscillations per second.

"Until the energy in the vocal waves of vibration balances with the power in compressed breath, you have no control over your voice. Like two people trying to walk on the rails of a railroad—by holding hands they balance each other. They must be inseparable." —Lamperti

---

COORDINATION

One must have a deep coordination of all aspects of the voice in order to find the successful balance of resonance and timbre.

After the reflex/motivation of the neurological system (mind) starts sending commands, all the breathing muscles are actuated. This sends the breath through the vibrator of the voice box (vocal folds), producing a fundamental tone. The mind then continues to control the breath through touch felt by "inside skin" tissues of the throat, mouth, and nose as the sound wave progresses through the resonating pharynx, activating secondary vibrators such as the false vocal cords and laryngeal collar and enhancing the tone. Finally, all within a second of the initial motivation, the articulators of the mouth shape the tone into recognizable sounds and are united with the sense of hearing, which anticipates and controls the results.

If any part of this process is uncoordinated, bad vocal habits and possible harm may come to the vocal apparatus, causing reduced efficiency of sound, timbre, and articulation. Therefore, the study and practice of good technique should be isolated to each of these areas until each step of the process is efficient and supports all other steps. The importance of a well-trained voice instructor is obvious in helping the singing student build this coordination.

TESSITURA

Tessitura (*Italian*, texture) refers to the color or quality of the voice and the most comfortable pitch range the singer is capable of. Along with the aspect of where the voice lies the best (low, medium, or high) one can determine a singer's voice classification. For example, a mezzo-soprano usually possesses a darker texture and lower comfortable pitch range than the higher, brighter soprano voice type. However, vowel quality, poor integration of the two registers (chest and head voice or falsetto), lack of technical skill, and vocal faults sometime obscure the "natural tessitura" of the voice, so it is a common mistake to prematurely classify a voice type before the singer has worked with a teacher to iron out those vocal problems.

Another common mistake made in respect to tessitura is to classify voices based solely on the range of the voice. Although range is a major part of it, texture and tessitura are the main elements in determining what determines a singer's vocal classification.

NOSE RESONANCE VS. NASALITY

Singers often mistake nose resonance with nasality in the tone. But there is a big difference between the two that can easily be explained.

> **Nose resonance** is a sympathetic vibration the singer feels behind the nose, or nasopharynx, when the vocal cords make sound. It is completely natural as a result of good acoustics in the mouth (especially a well-placed tongue and use of pure vowels).

> **Nasality** is a result of the singer's attempt to intentionally place those same sound vibrations into the nasopharynx, often in a

misguided attempt to increase resonance and a need to place the tone in the mask. It can also be the result of a pulled-back tongue, which sends the sound up into the sinuses instead of straight out the mouth. This is usually the result of impure vowel placement (Example: "uh" instead of "ah").

An easy way to determine whether nasality is a problem and affecting the sound is to pinch the nose closed with your fingers and sing a pitch on a vowel. If the fingers vibrate and the sound quality and/or pitch is affected, there is too much sound resonating in the nasopharynx. Now, try again, placing the sung pitch completely in the mouth and forward toward the lips and teeth, and then pinch your nose. If the fingers don't vibrate and the voice sounds the same, you're in the correct position. There is still sympathetic resonance in the nasopharynx, but this false resonance is not a major contributing factor to acoustic output.

The singer will find that with proper placement technique in the mouth they will be able to sing through nasal blockage caused by a common cold or allergies. Of course, because of the blockage they'll be less able to hear a ringing resonance in their mask and ears. At that point, it's important that the singer not force the voice or push more to compensate for the resonant feeling that is missing. The singer should trust that the acoustic work is being done in the throat and mouth, where, if they are engaging correct technique, there should be no negative effect on sound quality.

"The reverberations of the room are but enlarged reproductions of the vibration and resonance in the head and chest." —LAMPERTI

THE ACOUSTIC CAGE

To produce and maintain what I call the acoustic cage (the optimal acoustical space) and find the most resonant formant frequency (singer's formant) in the mouth, the singer must modify the length and size of the vocal tract. This is achieved by lowering the larynx, raising the soft palate, keeping the tongue out of the way, and engaging the lips in such a matter as will immediately produce a better resonance for any singer.

"Resonance is but the working of the law of radiation, not a physical effort. It is controlled at the lips." —LAMPERTI

ENGAGING THE LIPS

As Robert Cowart, a diction coach I worked with at the Manhattan School of Music, used to say, "There should be a little 'oo' in everything you sing." He wasn't talking about the actual "oo" sound, however. He was referring to the shape the lips make when producing the "oo" sound. It's a slight flaring (not puckered) position maintained behind all vowels and consonants. For example, the "ee" sound when placed in this position sounds like a German umlauted u or "ü." This very efficient method of consonant and vowel modification or "resonance tuning" places the sound in a forward position, thus minimizing the use of too much air and boosting the acoustic output of the voice. This position also makes any vowel a tall vowel (as many choir directors instruct) by lifting the soft palate and helping to lower the larynx, giving more resonant space to the vocal tract. The flaring of the lips also exposes some of the lower teeth and helps extend the vocal tract length, which helps the sound waveform complete its cycle, thus amplifying the sound.

This acoustical position of the "oo" lips, also called "corners" by great pedagogues such as Shirlee Emmons and Berton Coffin, is not, however, the natural position used when normally speaking and must be ingrained into the singer's muscle memory. This is done by practicing with conscious intent and monitoring of the lips (preferably in front of a mirror) to make sure they don't pull out of position or make the face look unnatural. Consistent forward placement of the lips in the "oo" position not only lowers formant frequencies in the vocal tract, it also enhances the lower harmonics by lowering the larynx and raising the soft palate, and produces a richer tone, maintains acoustical stability, and assures correct airflow. This consistent forward placement is much easier when singing vocalises on a single vowel and takes a consistent effort and much practice to achieve when used with text. How to connect with a song's text correctly to maintain acoustical stability will be covered more in Chapter Four of this book.

Personally, I have always found that my sound quality was more beautiful when I was singing in French. I always wondered why I got the role or placed in the competition when I auditioned with songs in that language. I later realized that spoken French precipitated a need to engage the lips more than other languages, so it was easier to maintain the placement when singing in French. It's easy to be lazy and uncommitted when speaking conversationally in any language. Unless we are speaking to someone across the room, trying to make a point, or are angry or emotional when speaking, there is not much engagement of the lips.

When singing, however, this noncommitment and lack of consistent placement contributes to the inability to maintain the correct acoustics and greatly lessens the resonance of the sound. Acoustically speaking, the lack of lip flare shortens the vocal tract, keeping the sound wave from completing, and by doing so causes a damping effect. When the singer pulls back his or her lips out of the "oo" position to smile, or when they complete words such as "when" or "tree" by pulling back their lips, it causes the correct acoustical resonance to spread and loose consistency.

To avoid coming out of position and spreading, practice in front of a mirror to make sure the lips don't pull back on certain words and only relax during moderate and extended rests and breaks (for quick breaths stay in position). Some singers feel they have to smile all the time onstage. This completely throws the acoustical positioning out of whack. Make sure to only spread into a full smile during moderate and extended rests and breaks. Smile with the eyes instead of the mouth while singing to avoid spreading vowels. Otherwise the quality of the sound is compromised.

Consistently engaging and ingraining the flared shape in the muscle memory of the lips takes a lot of practice but is well worth the time and patience. Much like a student who plays a brass or woodwind instrument, the lip muscles needed for a classical singer to achieve a proper acoustical sound take time and practice to strengthen. But by monitoring oneself in a mirror, and being very conscious of when the lips want to pull back out of position, the student will eventually build up their lip "chops," thus keeping the "acoustical cage" intact and allowing the voice to retain the consistent resonance and buzz needed to carry the voice out to the audience and dramatically improve sound quality.

"Slow [and fast] noiseless inhaling commences at the bottom and fills gradually toward the top, retaining the abdominal participation in the act. The diaphragm controls the exit of the breath to produce all sounds at all pitches." —LAMPERTI

INHALATION

To avoid changing the optimal acoustical shape of the vocal tract, the singer should always inhale in the same position as the phrase that follows it (See Chapter Three, "Throat position during Inhalation") and then continue singing behind the flared lip position through the entire phrase (monitor yourself in a mirror to make sure you look natural).

When there's no jaw tension, the ability to breathe in a low position is greatly enhanced and allows the singer to get on top of the pitch with the following consonants and vowels of the text, also in a low position. This allows for good resonance to be continually maintained in the vocal tract instead of lifting the larynx on a shallow breath and returning to the low position when singing the words.

TONGUE POSITION

The tongue should be relaxed, resting on the floor of the mouth with the tip against the back of the lower teeth to allow sound to efficiently reach the articulators (teeth, lips, jaw, and tip of the tongue). On open vowels, correct tongue position is either flat against the mouth floor or has a "v" or "u" shaped indentation running down the middle (check this out in a mirror). Wrong tongue position, often caused by tongue tension, is a major contributor to poor tone quality and inability to stay in tune. Vowels distort when the tongue is pulled back into the throat, producing a muddy sound and unclear diction. Remember, one should always think of what is going on acoustically in the mouth when singing. Keeping the sound waves from being dampened by a misplaced tongue is of primary consideration.

Vocal resonance is an important function of tongue positioning. Although the singer may not be conscious of it at the time, the tongue helps to keep vocal resonance consistently even from note to note by subtly adjusting its positioning. The tongue also allows the vocal tract to constantly change from pitch to pitch, so after building muscle memory through much practice the singer no longer has to search for the ideal positioning but allows the tongue to adjust to the correct acoustical form on its own. Any forced posture or manipulation of the tongue by the singer trying to superficially "cover" the tone or achieve more resonance changes the vocal tract adversely and can create tongue tension.

TONGUE TENSION

Emotion is stored in our muscles, and no more so than the tongue. Years of being told to "hold" or "bite" your tongue, aggression expressed through anger, faulty breast or bottle-feeding, or being "tongue-tied" (an oral anomaly called ankyloglossia, as seen in Appendix I) can cause much tension in the tongue. That's why tongue root tension can be the cause of so many vocal problems. Releasing extreme tongue root tension can be achieved by physical manipulation such as in regular tongue-stretching exercises usually done before warming up the voice. Here is one exercise that might help.

Open your mouth as wide as you can and stick your tongue out as far as possible and rock it from side to side. Repeat this exercise a number of times to help release the tension.

JAW POSITIONING

A wide jaw opening contributes directly to the raising of the first formant. This enhances the fundamental's amplitude, causing the sound to be larger. The opposite is true of a higher jaw opening. Since this position does not rise the first formant, a weakness of the sound is produced. Therefore, both consonants and vowels should always be approached with a lower jaw position. There is never a need for excessive jaw action. "Jawing" of words makes singing much more work and causes wide variations in acoustics, depriving the singer of a consistent resonant space in the mouth.

JAW TENSION

The essential need for a relaxed jaw cannot be emphasized enough. Many of us carry our tension in our jaws, so without releasing some of this tension before singing, the practice session or performance will never be acoustically satisfying. The looser the jaw, the more the throat is relaxed, and this helps to lower the larynx, which opens the vocal tract and creates a more beautiful resonance. The tighter the jaw, the higher the breath is produced in the chest or throat, making the sound tight and pushed. Although contemporary singing styles can get away with higher-placed positioning, classical singers need to connect to a lower source of breathing and a much more open throat, so they must be able to drop the jaw.

Before singing the singer should always stretch out and loosen the muscles of the jaw. One way to relieve jaw tension is to put a wine cork between the front teeth (cut to size if too large), letting the jaw muscles stretch out for three minutes or so. If you have TMJ (temporomandibular joint syndrome) and the jaw clicks and catches in front of the ear, do not try these stretches. After the jaw feels loose, place your finger on the condyle joint right in front of the earlobe and drop the jaw until the fingertip goes into a slight indentation. Sing through some scales on "ah" with your fingertips in the indentations and don't close the jaw enough to push your fingertips out, even when you breathe. Once you feel you can maintain this position, pull the fingers out of the indentations and sing through your repertoire, occasionally checking back with your fingertips.

RAISED SOFT PALATE/LOWERED LARYNX

Raising the soft palate and lowering the larynx are two main contributors to maximizing vocal resonance. Modifying the vocal tract in this fashion aligns the vocal tract, optimizes resonance, and enhances the whole spectrum of frequencies/formants/overtones needed to produce a large, well-rounded sound. This is achieved by a relaxed lower jaw, the feeling of the start of a yawn, and low support of the breath.

I often tell my students to impersonate the voice of a radio announcer and sing through that space. Or talk with a vampire accent. (Example: "I'm Count Chawkula, and I vawnt to drink your blawd.") This enhanced space in the vocal tract creates the larger, rounded, and deeper sound found in classical singing but can be used at times in musical theater or pop singing when the singer wants to warm up a certain sound or add spin or vibrato to the voice. (Example: A jazz singer may hold a straight tone and then relax the throat into a nice vibrato at the end of the note.)

I often demonstrate the difference of the two styles to my students. First, I'll sing a song for them in a musical theater style, singing the song as much like I would speak it in a stage voice as possible. Then I sing it in a classical, raised soft palate/lowered larynx position. I ask them to be very observant about how I breathe, what's happening with my mouth position, and what kind of space they think I feel in my vocal tract. There are several ways to find that correct raised soft palate/lowered larynx position to create an open-throated full resonance (called *gola aperta* in Italian) through the singer's entire range. When lowering the larynx, you may see that it's almost always performed in conjunction with raising the soft palate. This combination of movement gives the singer the ability to inhale volumes of air more quickly, enhances vocal efficiency, and sets up the appropriate vocal tract alignment.

Here are a few ways to find the correct alignment using the imagination. Some of these may already be familiar.

1. Smell the rose.
2. Begin to yawn.
3. Make an inward smile.

VOICE PERSONALITIES

We've all noticed the incredible resonance and vocal flexibility many radio personalities and voice-over talents have. How do you think that's created? These voice personalities have worked for years on their vocal identity. They grew up using their voices to imitate animal sounds or doing impersonations of people. They've "played" with and stretched their voices to their limits, and they know that the different spaces in their mouth and throat can be fine-tuned, through repetition, to do pretty much anything. Although every one of them has developed a repertoire of unique voices, they all have two things in common. They have great ears, and they consciously listen to nuances of sound and space. Personally, I'm amazed that many of these voices have not engaged in singing careers because they are basically finding the same space of resonance singers look for. But that shouldn't stop singers from imitating them. They've found something that we want, resonance, and through imitation (see more on imitation in Chapter Five) we can take what they have found into the singing arena.

As we've discussed throughout this chapter, it's all a matter of balance, of lifting the soft palate and lowering the larynx, used in conjunction with great diction and enunciation. Just for fun, try imitating a famous DJ or announcing voice.

Try saying "This is CNN" the way we hear it on TV. Besides having an amazing acting career, James Earl Jones is well known for his distinctly deep, authoritative voice, including on this announcement. First say the phrase in your normal speaking voice, then imitate Jones's voice as closely as possible. Feel the difference in your mouth and throat. What's going on in there? You've found the space in your throat that we just talked about a few paragraphs ago (low larynx and high soft palate). Now, while still enunciating the text (or any short sentence), keep that space and start slowly inflecting your speaking voice up and down. Basically, you are singing without set pitches. Once you have gotten the resonance and inflection you're looking for, start holding out pitches. See how this type of speech is so closely related to classical singing?

IMAGERY SCALE FOR DETERMINING A STUCK SOUND

When trying the DJ voice in the last exercise, did you hear and feel a stuck or muffled sound that sometime ended up in the nasal cavity? That's not only common when speaking in that space, it's what many singers do when trying to find the correct space. They feel that they have to pull the vowels back from their pure, in-the-lips position to where they think resonance lies. This illusion, that the placement they are looking for is made in the throat, causes a stuck sound and makes singing way too much work. Here is a qualitative scale I go by in determining how pure my sung vowels are and whether there is a propensity to pull back my vowels in order to find resonance.

> *Exercise: On a scale of 1 through 10, imagine 1 being cotton candy and 10 being the point of a sharp pencil. It's always good to sing the extremes or limits of the voice at least once to see where we are on this scale. When singing at 1 the sound is so muffled and covered you can hardly understand a word that's sung. When singing the number 10 the sound is screechy and pushed into the mask with bright vowels.*

What we're looking for as the perfect engagement of the vocal cords is around a number 8 on the scale. So, go to a 10 and make a pushed glottal "ee" sound (don't hurt yourself), then pull back to an 8. Now loosen the throat and while still keeping the placement of the 8 in your mouth and lips, lift the soft palate, lower the larynx, and sing a note with a nice low supported breath.

USING FALSETTO TO FIND CORRECT VOCAL TRACT PLACEMENT

For men, one of the most helpful techniques I have found (thank you, Craig Rutenberg) to help line up all vowels in the same resonant space is to first work a song or aria initially in its written octave, and then take the piece up an octave or so and work the aria in the falsetto range of the voice.

Of course, in order to get the most benefit out of this exercise, the male singer must already be adept at making a beautiful open resonance in their falsetto. Since there are two types of falsetto, one being pushed with a straight airy tone, and the other using a lifted soft palate and relaxed throat (creating as womanly a tone as possible), those singers unable to properly open into a relaxed falsetto will find this technique much less effective if not impossible to achieve. However, once learned, always keeping the feeling of a resonant falsetto while singing in the full voice will keep the vocal tract open, the soft palate up, and the larynx lowered.

This coordinated use of falsetto voice with the full (chest) voice is basically what *bel canto* calls "building on the soft," or singing softly with the feeling of a full falsetto resonance. In men this "mix" of falsetto is most fully engaged in their *passaggio* so they can extend their full voice at least three notes higher. In women their head voice is also engaged in this way with chest voice in their *passaggio* (prima).

"The sound of the word controls resonance and color. Coordinated breathing furnishes energy." —LAMPERTI

MARKING AND *SOTTO VOCE*

Similar to "building on the soft" is the ability to mark or sing in *sotto voce*. Marking is the ability to sing an aria or song with a)

the correct technique at the same intensity but half the volume (*sotto voce*), or b) an octave lower than normally sung. Both are used to spare the voice from too much wear, keeping the singer's voice fresh for performance. *Sotto voce* should be used in three different singing situations: as a voice-saving tool in rehearsals, as a blending tool for large operatic voices singing in a choir, and during personal practice.

When I started to take voice lessons in the ninth grade (after several years singing in choirs), my voice began to stand out in my bass section in choir. The more I developed my solo voice, the harder it was to rein in and mix the sound with the rest of the choir. Luckily, my voice teacher instructed me not to come off my support and decrease the sound to match the volume of the other singers in my section, an instruction not often given to large voices. But I did have to blend. So, until my late twenties I pulled back the vowels and sound into my throat and got into the habit of singing from a clogged or stuck position. Distorting my vowels affected my pitch, my range, my volume, and my diction, and this really became apparent as a soloist. Unfortunately, we didn't catch this progressively growing bad habit at the time.

It took another ten years working with university and private voice teachers before I was able to pull the sound out of the back of the throat, learn to ride the breath in a forward, balanced placement, and sing *sotto voce* in choirs with the energy and freedom I used in my full operatic voice.

CROSSOVER—TO LIFT OR NOT TO LIFT

All of my voice teachers have been classically trained, as was I, in the *bel canto* method. Therefore, I had always taught my beginning students with a classical technique that focuses on how to breathe correctly, the use of pure vowels, correct posture, etc. These are essential elements in singing any genre of music, however, and much like studying ballet builds a dancer's solid foundation for other dance forms such as jazz and modern, a classical singing technique sets the foundation for all styles of singing.

As explained earlier, most beginning voice students singing in a classical style are often not as discerning about singing pure vowels as they should be (Example: "uh" instead of "ah" or "ih" instead of "ee"). They just know that they want to sound a little louder and maybe a little more mature than their current age. Therefore, they often place the sound back in the mouth and by the ears, where they can hear it better. But this is regrettably also where the sound wave hits soft tissue and is dampened. This is why many classical students find it hard to cross over to musical theater and pop. They don't have the right placement and enough articulation in their lips. This causes their vowels to be distorted and unnatural sounding. Not conversational enough.

When I started teaching more and more musical theater students, I noticed that most of them had good breath support (for stage voice projection) and actually engaged their lips when they sang, which helped them retain pure and understandable vowel placement. I'd been taught to use my actor's "stage voice" when I was earning my BFA in theater and voice at the University of Kansas and had developed a strong, open-throated approach to speaking that was supported with low breath support. I suspected this was the very reason I was personally more adept to crossing over between vocal styles than most of my opera colleagues (that and singing in rock bands in high school). Actors were more concerned about being understood and projection than making a big resonant sound. So, I decided to start teaching my beginning voice students differently.

I began emphasizing placement and engagement of the lips, as well as the meaning of the text, before teaching space and resonance. This achieved quicker results. Instead of working resonance technique at the beginning, I realized they had to first learn how to speak effectively.

When I gave my theater students a classical piece to work on, I noticed that they retained the pure vowels, even singing in other languages. Yes, they would at first sing the art song or aria in a less resonant musical theater style, but they could be understood because the text was placed in the lips. And they were much faster to adapt the technique of raising the soft palate and lowering the larynx to increase resonance than my classical student's ability to keep the right vowel placement and sound natural when they were given a musical theater piece to work on. Therefore, I believe all beginning students benefit highly from learning musical theater pieces or English art song first before starting into those 24 Italian Songs and Arias.

COVERING

The term "covering" seems to pop up when speaking of two different aspects of singing. Although not entirely unrelated, there should be some distinction made between the two meanings. The first refers to a popular remedy to navigate through the *passaggio*, where we find that deliberately making small adjustments in vowels helps with the transition between registers. For example, modifying the vowel "ah" a little toward "oh" helps to change the length and thickness of the vocal folds, making them longer and thinner. In doing so, the act of covering energizes the low formants, thus minimizing the use of the chest voice and increasing the use of the falsetto or head voice.

Covering can also be defined as the position change or expansion that takes place in the pharynx between the true vocal cords and the false vocal cords, as in the feel of yawning, that causes the voice to sound darker. This, in combination with engaged "oo" lips, modifies the vowel "ee" to an umlauted "ü" sound and causes the larynx to lower, helping achieve the desirable sound we look for in operatic and classical singing.

The concept of covering is often misunderstood. In the Italian model it is a well-balanced vowel resonance based on subtle vocal timbre adjustments that produce a "closed voice," in contrast to a yell-like "open voice" at the top of an ascending line. However, the German concept of covering is often associated with abrupt vocal adjustments that can cause the upper covered tones to sound heavy and dark, with pressure in the throat.

An appropriate covering uses both the sensation in the mask and hard palate for frontal resonance while singing in the closed vowel position. This forward, high-placed, and focused position should be consistently used in conjunction with lowering the jaw to a comfortable position, all while keeping the tongue relaxed. When singing from low to high ranges, this covering technique allows the appropriate vowel modification needed to produce a consistently free tone.

VOWEL PLACEMENT

Although we will also be talking about vowel placement in Chapter Four, we must first make sure the vowel does not inhibit the resonance of the voice because of impurity or misplacement. Improper vowel placement is a main contributor to:

1. Poor acoustical resonance (directing tone into the nasal cavities and/or soft tissue damping)
2. Slow development of the upper range
3. Being flat in pitch
4. Pushing
5. Poor diction

It is important to clean up this problem as soon as possible if there is to be any major improvement of the voice. The great early

Italian voice teachers of *bel canto* understood this and had their students study at least one hour a day for years on specifically cleaning up poor vowel diction. Some of the reasons for improper vowel placement while singing include:

1. A misplaced or tense tongue (see tongue tension earlier this chapter)
2. Disengaged lips
3. Poor speaking skills or poor understanding of a language's pronunciation (see IPA in Chapter Four)
4. Inability to hear the difference between pure and distorted vowels
5. Incorrect onset placement

"A focused vowel is the most difficult to control. Because it must start like a needle puncture, expand into full resonance and disappear into silence, without undue effort, and no escape of air, other than to feed the vibration." —LAMPERTI

WEIGHT IN THE VOICE

How many times have you heard the term "weight" when related to the voice? The term is usually associated with what kind of flow of air is being used. When the vocal folds are phonating, does the sound come up and out of the mouth with no control, or is there something controlling that flow of air? Are some kind of glottal and placement mechanisms, such as vocal cords and articulators (lips, teeth, and tongue), working to help control how fast and exacting the air is released?

Much like the opening of a full balloon has to be unpinched incrementally to keep the air from escaping too quickly, the singer has to find a fine balance when controlling the release of air through the glottis (space between the vocal folds). The glottis can't be too tight or pinched (stopping the sound), or too relaxed, allowing too little resistance and causing the air to fall out and the torso to collapse.

Often the young student will not be connecting with their vocal folds enough, causing a wispy, hollow sound that loses far too much air. This is often the case with young choral singers. Remedies for this problem are found in Chapter Three, particularly with "The Monkey" and "Barn Door" exercises.

RESONANCE EXERCISES

Much of the following exercises, designed to help in the development of resonance and optimal acoustics, deals with vowel placement and should always be done in conjunction with the formula dictating that 95 percent of the sound made should be placed on the vowel, and 5 percent of the sound made on the consonant. Also, engagement of the lips in the "oo" position, as indicated through much of this book, is important and will again be covered.

A lowered larynx (voice box), in conjunction with a raised soft palate, is used in classical singing much more than any other singing style and helps create resonant space in the lower pharynx (vocal tract). With my students I've often compared this action with that of turning up the bass on a stereo system equalizer, which engages a speaker's "woofer."

When the larynx isn't lowered, the voice has fewer lower frequencies/formants. Just singing from the throat and chest and not dropping the larynx and engaging low breath support produces a much smaller sound and only engages the "tweeter" and "midrange." The more the singer engages the "woofer," the deeper and rounder, or classical sounding, the voice appears. Therefore, one must conclude that a major element dictating appropriate vocal style is the correct amount of "space" in the vocal tract, or how low the larynx is (Example: Low larynx for classical, higher larynx for contemporary styles). Here are exercises that help lower the larynx and open the throat. It's always best to get in front of a mirror to monitor your progress:

A Loose, Lowered Jaw #1

At the start of your daily singing practice regimen, the first thing to do is loosen the jaw. This free jaw helps lower the breath support, relaxes the throat, and lowers the larynx. Without this preparation your practice time will be much less effective. A couple of ways to loosen the jaw include:

Stretching the mouth open as wide as possible, holding it there for five seconds, and then closing the mouth in a type of chewing motion. (I call this "gross chewing.") Do this at least five times, occasionally sticking your tongue out as far as possible and rocking it back and forth sideways to also loosen the tongue.

A Loose, Lowered Jaw #2

Take a wine cork and cut it down to fit how wide the mouth opens. Put it between the front teeth and let it keep the jaw open and stretched for approximately two minutes. Just like what happens when one stretches a spring too far, when the cork is taken out the mouth should feel very "slack jawed" and not snap back.

Using a relaxed jaw and breathing deeply into the lower support is accomplished much easier as a result of a lowered larynx. It relaxes the throat and opens the space in the lower pharynx. The incorrect approach includes a tight jaw and breathing from the chest and throat, which keeps the larynx high, denying the singer access to the resonance needed for classical singing.

Posture

Alignment is important in maintaining a lowered larynx. Keep the shoulders dropped, sternum up, back of the neck stretched, feet solid into the ground with a loose jaw and face.

Low Vowels

Use low vowels to find the lower larynx position. Then incorporate that same feeling behind all the vowels and consonants you sing.

A few vowels to practice with include: "oo," "oh," "ah," "uh," and "aw." Notice how the lips on these vowels make the flared-lip position I've talked about so much in this book? Without the "oo" lips behind everything we sing, there is the rise of the larynx and lessening of sound quality.

"Stroking the Beard"

Monitor the "oo" position by taking either one or both hands and with the fingers stroke down, on both sides of the mouth, to the bottom of the jaw. This reminds yourself to make and maintain a lowered jaw position.

Paper Towel Tube

An excellent way to remind yourself to keep the low vowel position and "oo" lips is by singing down the middle of a cardboard paper towel tube (don't touch the tube with the mouth) through your entire song or aria. No tube? Take a pencil and pretend it has a bigger opening and sing down the middle of that.

Finger above the Adam's Apple

(This works only with men.) Once the larynx is lowered, a good way to monitor its position through the phrase is to put your index finger horizontally against the neck above the Adam's apple and keep it there through the whole song. Monitor when the Adam's apple pops above the finger. This should only happen when the singer swallows or has a rest of more than a couple of beats. Otherwise, the finger should always be on the top of the Adam's apple, even when breathing.

Pillars of the Throat
In this exercise one is teaching the throat to compensate for the clamping effect that wants to occur naturally when ascending to a higher note. Pretend that there are two pillars in your throat. First, put your hands together as if praying (fingers straight up and parallel to each other). Then, after a nice low breath, start with an "ah" vowel on a low note and glide up an octave, gradually pulling the hands apart while imagining the two pillars in the throat are widening. This stretch lifts the soft palate and lowers the larynx. (Never pull in the stomach and reach for the note with your throat!)

Rubber Band/Bungee Cord
Very similar to the last exercise, this allows a feeling of stretch in the throat while ascending to a higher note. Using a real or imaginary thick rubber band or bungee cord, stretch (or pretend to stretch) the cord while taking a deep, low breath by pulling up with one hand and down with the other as you glide from a low to high note on an "ah" vowel. This stretch loosens the throat, drops the larynx, and keeps the breath support low.

On the Edge
This is the simplest way to find the low larynx position. Feeling like you are just on the edge of a yawn puts you in the perfect position. To monitor and maintain this position while singing, take the index fingers of both hands and put the tips in the open jaw socket indentations in front of the earlobes. If the jaw is loose enough it will not be hard to find. By keeping the finger firmly in that indentation,

even while breathing, the loose placement of the jaw will be assured, and the larynx lowered throughout the phrase.

Having covered most of the aspects of good resonance in this chapter, you should now understand the importance of the space and shape of the vocal tract in determining the appropriate acoustics and timbre of the voice, the balance between the forward placement of vowels in coordination with an open throat (*chiaroscuro*), and the different registers of the male and female voice. None of this means anything, however, if the source behind the voice, or the breath, has insufficient intent to keep the tone solidly connected. In the next chapter we'll be covering the importance of balanced breath, its correct onset and release, and focus of the breath and its overall coordinated management. We'll also explore the importance of *appoggio* and some fun vocal exercises that help make it work.

THREE

The Breath Connection

"Difficulties in singing come from three directions: uneducated hearing, undisciplined muscles and untrained breathing."
—Lamperti

Although normal breathing is essentially automatic, to meet the artistic requirements to sing a song efficiently the singer must be able to modify at will the ability to fill and empty the lungs quickly, slowly, forcefully, or gently to achieve the volume and pitch of the vocal sound desired. But most importantly, they must be able to find the right "balance" of air when singing. Therefore, before vocal production is attempted, the student should acquire a method of breath management.

In this chapter I will not discuss at length the physiology of the breathing apparatus. I will, however, look at how to manage, balance, excite, and connect the breath. Many high school singers and beginning vocal majors in college have developed inefficient breathing habits as a result of little prior individual vocal study and/or bad choral habits they have developed over the years. Because they've bypassed any pre-vocal training (i.e., learning how to breathe), they've never learned the correct way to inhale and release the breath into the musical phrase. For most beginners and singers with poor breathing habits, the breath is mistakenly taken high in the chest, held there, and then released from a held position. As a result, the sound is pushed and tight, and often causes pitch problems and clumsy onsets of tone, attacks, and releases.

Most untrained singers breathe with the same intensity as if they are speaking because the process of breathing is usually taken for granted. However, when singing, the demands to finely tune musical phrasings, dynamic levels, and vocal registers with varied levels of intensity and frequency variations require knowledge of breath support/management as well as specific laryngeal adjustments. The ability to either breathe quickly or slowly is essential. And much like an athlete, the regulated and coordinated breathing of a singer is only achieved through many hours of exercise and practice. The correct breathing skills needed to fulfill the artistic requirements of the music also reward the singer with positive physiological side effects, such as an increase in physical strength, acute awareness, and concentration. Research shows that correct breathing is also a natural antidepressant that creates hormones such as oxytocin, to alleviate stress and anxiety, and endorphins, associated with feelings of pleasure (Chicago Tribune, 2018).

"Only when tone seems part of bone and muscle of the head will energy flow from all parts of the body to produce compressed breath that feeds it." —LAMPERTI

MANAGEMENT AND CONNECTION

Correct breath management uses a combination of the following:

1. Consistent and balanced breath support
2. A relaxed and open vocal tract

3. Correct tongue placement
4. Forward placement of pure vowels and consonants
5. Appropriate engagement of the lips

The acoustics within the mouth and throat produced by this coordination will dictate how free or constricted the airflow will be, and regular practice will help build the muscles in the lower diaphragm for the even regulation of that airflow. If the singer finds they are pushing or that singing is too much work, the problem is a lack of breath or airflow coordination in some part of the singing apparatus. Here are two ways to help correct these coordination problems:

Correct Intake and Release of the Breath. Relaxing and dropping the jaw opens the throat so the singer can access their lower breath support. The opposite is true when there is too high a jaw and too small a mouth during inhalation. This tightness of the jaw causes the singer to breathe from their chest or throat, creating a shallow and pushed release of air through the glottis. Therefore, always insist on stretching out the jaw before singing. I find that the wine cork method discussed in Chapter Two works well, or if no cork is available, just stretch the mouth open as far as possible and hold. Rubbing the jaw's joint muscles in front of the ears with your fingers also helps relax the muscles.

Next, put your hands on your stomach above the belt line. Breathe deep and feel your hands pushed outward. Now, while keeping the chest up and shoulders back, release (not push) and fall into the tone, keeping that forward support against your hands. See how long you can hold that note without letting the stomach or chest cave in. Continue this exercise in front of a mirror to make sure the shoulders do not rise and the chest does not lift. The student may find this exercise easier lying on their back on the floor with a heavy book on their stomach. It takes a while to train the muscles to breathe in this fashion, but it is necessary to breathe low to connect with the support needed. (See *appoggio* later in this chapter.)

Engaging Pure Vowels. Engaged lips help keep pure vowels from distorting and falling back in the mouth. All too often the singer mistakenly thinks that pulling back the vowel creates a larger, or in choral situations, a more blended sound. In this misshaping of the vowel, for example, the vowel "ee" is sung as "ih" or "ah" is sung as "uh" and directs the airflow into soft tissue, where it dampens the sound and ends the sound wave. This results in a stuck or muffled sound.

I've found this is a major problem prevalent primarily in young singers, but to a degree it can be found in many experienced singers as well. Finding a pure vowel is very elusive and hard for the student to hear. Personally, I always had a problem finding a pure "oo" sound. But I especially find about 90 percent of beginning students have problems with a pure "ah," often deferring to the stuck "uh" position.

The teacher should constantly insist on the purity of the vowel sound during the lesson. Students, while in personal practice, should also pay close attention to the engagement of the lips while standing in front of a mirror. As detailed in Chapter Two, a small consistent fluting of the lips ("oo" lips) behind pure vowels (and consonants) controls airflow, lifts the soft palate, and lowers the larynx, making the tone much rounder and more resonant. With persistent practice, producing as pure a vowel as possible and singing all text in a forward position drastically enhances airflow management to create a much more free and balanced sound.

NOSE vs. MOUTH INHALATION

The singer has the choice of intaking air by either the nose or mouth. Although there are benefits to both ways, my preference, especially in classical and opera singing, is using the mouth or a combination of both the nose and mouth in succession.

Because the nose is used to filter particles and produce nitric oxide to enhance oxygen intake, there are many health benefits to this form of breathing, such as strengthening the immune system and improving memory and concentration. However, when the singer needs to take a quick, low breath, the nose is not large enough to intake enough air to lower the diaphragm sufficiently to support the vocal line. There is also the chance that the nose may be stuffed up at the time, which will slow down the intake of air considerably. Although I sometimes use a combination of both nose and mouth when inhaling slowing, starting with the nose first and opening into the mouth, it really depends on how fast the breath is inhaled.

RHYTHMIC BREATHING

When starting a regular ascending phrase, the breath should be inhaled at the rate equivalent to the length of the note starting the phrase. Also, the faster the tempo, the more the mouth should be used to inhale. For example:

> **Whole Note:** if the tempo is slow with a beginning whole note, the breath is inhaled for four beats in the tempo of the music, with the first two beats inhaled by the nose and expanding into an open throat/mouth breath at the third and fourth beat before dropping the breath into the phrase. Never hold the breath between inhalation and phonation! The duration of dropping the air into the tone is quite short, usually the length of an eighth to a quarter note, much like an exasperated sigh.

Dotted Half Note: if the tempo is slow, inhale the same way as the whole note only with less time in the nose.

Half Notes: inhale through just the mouth for two beats in the tempo of the music.

Quarter Notes and all shorter notes: take a low, quick eighth note breath using just the mouth to inhale.

When starting the phrase on a high note, the onset should always be started with a low, quick breath through the mouth, allowing the singer to get on top of the starting pitch. Never hold the breath between inhalation and onset!

"Silent breathing should be the rule except for emotional effect. If the singer wishes to secure diaphragmatic and abdominal control of his breath, he himself must not hear the inrush of the breath." —LAMPERTI

THROAT POSITION DURING INHALATION

The ability to breathe as quickly and deeply as possible is a great asset to the singer in energizing and supporting the sound. In order to do this, the throat should always be in an open and loose position, with the soft palate up and larynx lowered (see Chapter Two on "Inhalation"). Since this is the same position as during phonation, and since it is completely different from the way we speak (where we start phonating from a glottal onset and collapse between sentences), this open-throated breath position is not a reflex that comes naturally and has to be taught. These exercises have proven helpful:

Jaw and Breath. To ingrain this breath position into the muscle memory, the singer should concentrate before every vocalization on keeping the jaw loose (feeling close to a yawn) and breathe into the lower support. Then (never hold the breath between inhalation and release) let the breath fall into the notes of the exercise, as if in a sigh (see "Falling into the Breath" later in this chapter). After phonating, remember to inhale in the same position before starting the next exercise or phrase. You may have to occasionally swallow, but always breathe while keeping the mouth and throat open.

Big Fog vs. Small Fog. Do you remember when you were a kid riding in the backseat of the family car making a fog with your breath on a cold window? You wanted to make the fog big enough to write and draw on. The more open your throat when you inhaled, the deeper the breath. If you left your throat in a open position and exhaled slowly on the surface, the fog would be really big. This is the throat position you should always use in classical singing. It lifts the soft palate, lowers the larynx, puts the breath into your lower support, and creates a resonant sound when exhaling on a tone. Repeat this over and over to get used to this feeling so the muscles always know where to go when inhaling and exhaling.

PHONATION

The effectiveness of subglottal breath pressure against the vibrator (vocal folds) is determined by an aerodynamic factor called the Bernoulli Principle. This discovery, made in 1738 by Swiss scientist Daniel Bernoulli, explains how the lungs and diaphragm send air (breath support) up the trachea to press against the elastic muscles of the closed vocal folds, where the pressure causes them to part slightly, allowing a tiny amount of air to escape through the glottis (space between the folds). The vocal folds are immediately sucked back together, the subglottal air builds up against the folds again, and the effect repeats itself up to 2,000 times every second. This succession of glottal cycles creates a sound wave that travels up through the vocal tract, is enhanced by the air-filled cavities of the resonator (vocal tract) into a recognizable vocal tone, and is then modified into speech or sung text by the articulators (tongue, jaw, hard palate, lips, and teeth).

If your attack is too hard, you are hitting your tone from beneath your throat instead of focusing it above the vocal-cords. You are 'striking the glottis' instead of attacking your tone." —LAMPERTI

Onset of Tone

The way phonation is initiated (onset) will dictate how well the subsequent phrase will be sustained and influenced. According to which language you are singing, there is an appropriate way to use these onsets, but in general one is looking to use as coordinated an onset as possible. There are three types of onsets used when starting a phrase:

> **Glottal** (hard): This is sometimes referred to as singing from a held position and happens almost always when the phrase starts with a vowel. After breath pressure is built up under the glottis, the strongly closed vocal folds then explode apart, making an abrupt start to the vowel, which almost always causes phonation through the entire following phrase to be tense or pressed. A dramatic situation causing an emotional outburst (whether

by mistake or on purpose) may be one reason for this type of onset. Though a small amount of glottal onset is required in languages such as German and English, glottal onset in Italian and French is minimal.

Aspirate (soft): Too much airflow at the onset of the tone results anytime the singer uses an "h" to initiate the tone. Though this is natural in singing words that begin with this consonant or its sound equivalent, too much airflow through vocal folds that aren't properly adducted will cause breathy or aspirate phonation through the whole phrase and cause the singer to run out of air prematurely and a deterioration of forward movement.

Coordinated (balanced): This is the type of onset all singers strive for. As I will explain later in the "Falling into the Breath" section, the need to equalize the breath above and below the glottis (opening between the vocal folds) before phonation is essential. Therefore, the movement of air before singing the first note in the phrase, much like a sigh, or the use of double consonants (see Chapter Four) keeps the singer from singing from a held and pushed position.

QUICK BREATH BEFORE ONSET

What happens when you start a phrase on a vowel? Especially one that starts on a high pitch? Although vowels are glottal in nature, starting the phrase need not start from a held position. The singer can avoid a hard-glottal onset by keeping the throat in the same relaxed, open position that the breath is taken. Here are a few ways to develop this quick breath technique:

Open Feeling. Take a low breath as fast as possible through a relaxed and open throat with no stopping to set—very important—before making the tone. Then, when exhaling to phonate, the singer should keep this open feeling in the throat as if they are still taking a breath. This allows the soft palate to stay up and the larynx to stay low during phonation, avoiding a grabbing or hard-glottal onset.

This quick breath (about a 1/16 note length) is most effective before the onset of vowels starting on a high pitch and may take some time to perfect. But for those who sing in choirs and have learned to stagger their breathing through a phrase, it should come faster.

The Cry/Welp. Pretend you're crying and feel how, after the cry deflates the lungs, the breath pops back in and starts another cry. When actually crying this can go on for a long time and is interspersed with short, quick jags or longer wails. Now, notice how the inhalations sometimes grab the cords and make a sound. What you want to do when pretending to cry is start getting used to that quick breath feeling, only make sure you have an open throat and breathe as low as possible to avoid the intake noise made in the real cry.

The Long Tone. Just like the staggered breathing used in choirs, sing a vowel as long as possible before taking a quick breath to continue the tone. Take a quick (1/16 note length) low breath with an open throat. Practice until you barely hear the break and you always land on the same pitch. Try using the "Flaring" technique in the "Release of Tone" section of this chapter.

Spiking the Volleyball. Pretend you're spiking a volleyball over the net by flipping the hands back on the quick breath and smacking the ball down with your fingers on the tone. When using this exercise to attack high notes, the quicker the breath the better. This gets you on top of the note so you can come down on it instead of pushing it. Notice the difference. If you take a slower breath (slower than 1/16), there is a stoppage after the breath, a setting up, and then a push on the onset of the tone. The soft palate is too low and the throat grabs as it pushes, thinning out the tone and losing the resonance.

PLAYING THE VOICE

Instrumentalists depress keys, strings, and valves to sound a note. Singers don't have that advantage. But they are able to use body movements to help learn singing techniques. Breath coordination and the onset of the note can be developed much faster if we use the hand and arm as a visual and tactile aid representing what is happening inside the body. Using arm and hand movements gives the singer a sense of coordination with the breath, instills the feeling of exact placement, helps with the feeling of forward movement, and encourages the whole body to be part of the singing process. Later, when performing in front of others, we can then internalize the process and sing with confidence and control without using these visual and tactile aids.

"When your tone emerges from silence into sound without effort, focused yet free, with sufficient energy to release, or restrain, back of it, you are one of the greatest singers."
—*LAMPERTI*

RELEASE OF TONE

Much like the onset, there must also be a balanced or coordinated release of sound at the end of the phrase. Releases can be produced in four ways:

Soft Release (aspirate). With this, the singer does not continue the forward movement to the last syllable, resulting in a breathy tone quality and collapsing of the breathing apparatus at the end of the phrase. This lack of intensity to the very end of the phrase causes the singer to "fall off the breath."

Hard Release (glottal). Here the singer halts the airflow in a type of "grunt." This type of release is rarely used, and only for dramatic effect in a performance by a large-voiced operatic singer.

Balanced Release. This is what we are looking for when ending a phrase—an even tension of the vocal folds after a consistent tone through the whole phrase. This release is similar to relaxed laughter.

Flaring. I have personally found another type of release, which I call flaring, to be the best option when singing with high energy and dramatic effect. Although the singer should already be leaning into the phrase (*appoggio*), flaring is a quicker lean into the support on the very last word (or couple of beats) of the phrase, and before the next breath. Though it should not be obvious to the listener, this extra kick into the lower breath support at the end of the phrase helps the singer expel the remaining breath, causing an automatic rather than intentional next breath. This reflex breath allows the outside air pressure to enter the body quickly and the energy of the song to move forward. Quick breathing is essential in both choral and solo singing. This flaring method, therefore, is a major breathing technique that helps in energizing the breath, maintaining breath support, sustaining good pitch, maintaining proper acoustic placement, and keeping the singer riding the breath with a forward momentum through the line.

BEAUTIFUL SINGING

> *"The focus of tone is like the converging rays of the burning lens. So intense is this 'point' that it is felt wherever it reaches. The glottis is the 'lens.' Compressed breath-energy is the 'sun.'"*
> —LAMPERTI

FOCUS AND PLACEMENT

Focus can be summarized as the maximized vibrational sensations of an efficiently produced vocal tone. It is often referred to as being vocally "hooked up." Tone quality can either be distorted and fuzzy or it can have focus. That focus, in conjunction with localized vowel placement (pure vowels), is produced by efficient vocal cord closure, enhanced by reflective sound sources of an acoustically aligned vocal tract, and perceived by the singer as sensations and vibrations.

Where these vibrations of acoustic pressure are sensed specifies the placement of the sound, and they often occur in the "mask" (around the nose, between the eyes and in the forehead) and behind the upper teeth on the hard palate. So, instead of listening for the best sound, the singer must "feel" the internal sensation of placement to be assured of the maximum resonance focus produced, also known as "ring" or "buzz" (*squillo*).

FALLING INTO THE BREATH

Control of airflow begins when the singer allows the breath to fall out of the mouth as in an exasperated sigh, releasing excess air on an "h" or a double soft consonant, causing the cords to immediately close, engage the tone, and start the phrase (see Chapter Four, "Double Consonants at Beginning of Phrases"). By doing so the singer equalizes the air pressure below and above the glottis so as to avoid singing from a held position. However, it more importantly helps the body engage with the tone.

This fall into the breath is similar to Lamperti's principle of "Breath before Tone," which is so helpful in finding healthy closure of the vocal folds.

An example of this would be to start a hum after puffing air (strongly) through the nose. This exercise immediately engages the body's lower diaphragm and the vocal folds and is a major component of efficient air management.

The need to equalize the breath above and below the glottis (opening between the vocal folds) before phonation is important for balanced sound production. But when too much air is dropped before phonation it may leave the singer with too little breath for the phrase and deterioration of forward movement. It is all a matter of coordinating the "fall" or "surrender" of the breath through the vocal folds, followed by a supported and balanced phonation. This fine balance between too little versus too much is only accomplished through vigilant practice.

"Energy must not become effort." —LAMPERTI

MORE BREATH EXERCISES

Balancing the Breath

The following exercise equalizes the breath above and below the glottis, releases tension to avoid pushing, and coordinates the exact way to approach the onset of tone. The four steps should be executed in order.

Inhale: With the tongue placed loosely against the bottom teeth and lying flat on the floor of the mouth, the throat in a relaxed yawning position, and jaw dropped, take a deep, low breath (no shoulders please) while lifting the arm at the elbow (finger pointing) at the same speed as the inhalation.

Exhale: Without stopping to hold the breath (very important), let the air drop out on the "h" of "hah," as if in a sigh, followed by a free fall of the hand and arm (don't control the fall). Try this a number of times before going on to the next step. Be careful to keep the throat relaxed and not grab the air with the throat as you release. If you do, you will feel a grabbing in your throat and hear a "white noise" sound before you hit the note.

Phonate: At the bottom of the arm and hand's free fall, let your finger snap forward at the exact time the vowel is sounded (on an "ah," not "uh"). This "whip" of the finger will ensure the coordinated onset of the vocal cords much as when the finger comes down on a key of a piano. (Onset, or the way the tone is initiated, is explained in detail in Chapter Four.) In fact, I suggest touching a table or surface with this snap technique so that there is a tactile reference ensuring exactness of glottal onset. Repeat this step by using different first consonants such as "mah" or "shah." (Let the "m" or "sh" sound while dropping your finger, then start the sound on "ah.")

Sustain tone: Repeating John Stephens's advice quoted earlier, "You don't make a tone, you release a tone." So, after learning to fall into the breath by repeating the above action over and over, let the air fall (release), snap the finger to the table, and sustain the tone. After the tone starts, continue to stay in that same open-throated "ah" position and think down and forward to the end of the note or phrase. If your throat is relaxed with the soft palate raised and the larynx lowered, the sound should start to "spin," causing a nice even vibrato. The exact opposite happens when the singer tries to "make" the tone by pushing the air. The chest and/or throat will tighten, and this will cause the sound to have a strained, straight tone. There is a fine balance between too much and too little breath to support an open-throated approach to singing. But this will be accomplished with practice.

You can also demonstrate this technique using common sports movements used in Frisbee, tennis, fishing, baseball, golf, or anything using these three basic movements.

Frisbee

- Pull back the throwing arm while breathing low and with an open throat.
- Pretend to throw the Frisbee with a quick release of air through an open throat. The action feels most like an exasperated sigh. Be sure not to push. If you incorrectly push the air out from your chest you will hear white noise and feel pressure in the throat. Keep upright with shoulders back. By letting the breath fall like a sigh you should feel the air react as if someone kicked out your knees from behind. This is when the tone starts.
- When you start singing the tone (at the "snap" of the throw) keep the open throat and support the breath by thinking low, out, and forward to the very end of the tone.

Tennis (Backhand Swing)

- Bring back the imaginary racket while taking in a low breath and open throat.
- Swing the racket while releasing the air through the same open throat.
- Connect the racket to the ball at the same time the air connects with the vocal cords. You should feel a low abdomen kick-out when you connect.

- Then support, support, support the note to the very end as you follow through with the imaginary racket. Keep the air excited and forward moving by thinking to the end of the note (or phrase).

Skipping the Rock/Belly Laughing

This exercise is similar to the two above, but this time we're engaging the vocal cords in a series of fast pulses. This is a great exercise to practice strengthening melismatic and coloratura passages.

Pretend you're standing on the shore of a lake. You have a nice flat rock in your hand, and you're going to try to skip it on the surface of the water as many times as possible. Put the rock between your thumb and first finger, pull back your arm, and throw, causing the rock to skip about four times before sinking beneath the surface. Now take that same motion, inhaling low as the arm is pulled back. Without hesitation throw the arm and an open-throated "h" forward and snap the rock from your fingers as you hit an "ah" vowel followed by multiple "hah hah hahs," making many skips and riding the sound until you run out of air. Notice how similar it is to a belly laugh. While practicing these even skips of sound on a relaxed throat, remember to keep the sternum high and always breathe from the lower diaphragm. Once you have learned this exercise, start using a metronome for evenness and speed, coordinating the skips of the rock to the beats of the metronome.

Exciting the Breath: Fogging the Mirror

A quick breath before a phrase is important in energizing the breath. As explained above, the throat must be in a relaxed open position (gola aperta), with the larynx lowered and soft palate up, so as much air as possible can be inhaled into the lower support as quickly as possible, much like a gasp. Here is a way to find that open throat position.

To get the gola aperta feeling of space that is needed, let's once again talk about Big Fog versus Small Fog. Stand close to a mirror or window and make a fog on its surface. If the fog is small, the singer has taken in too high a breath. The throat was not loose and open enough. You can tell the breath was too high by the amount of white noise made when inhaling. Now try to make as large a fog as you can on the surface. One should feel a loose and open yawny sensation in the throat. The jaw is dropped, causing the soft palate to be up and larynx down, and the air is drawn into the lower diaphragm. Now, slowly release the air, with the throat in the same position and lower support staying extended instead of collapsing. Make as little noise as possible during the exhale. Watch the fog fill the entire mirror. This is where the throat should be when inhaling a quick breath and pretty much at all times when singing classically.

Use this throat position to take a quick excited breath and attack the phrase (by quickly releasing the air) with intent and attitude. Just as an actor would study the meaning of the text to put themselves into the role of the character they are portraying, a singer also needs to find the motivation behind everything they sing and let the sound fly with abandon. Even if it is just a vocal exercise, they must pretend there is an emotional motivation that always keeps them moving forward through the phrase. This motivation excites the breath and maintains the support needed to sing long phrases with musicality and finesse.

Three other factors that help maintain an excited and supported breath and are usually not a natural aspect of intent or attitude are the use of double consonants, shadow vowels, and flaring at the end of phrases, all explained elsewhere in this book.

> *"If preparing to sing does not straighten you up like a soldier, some essential part of your anatomy is not taking part."*
> —LAMPERTI

SUPPORTING THE BREATH

If the student doesn't understand what breath support means, they are apt to think it means more air, while actually breath support equals less air. This is because breath support is the physical resistance the singer needs while exhaling. Everyone can exhale, but the singer has to resist the exhaled breath (demonstrated by using the Straw Technique that follows), thus building the singer's breath management. The *appoggio*, which is at the heart of the *bel canto* style, can help with several vocal problems a singer may have. Some of these problems include:

1. Taking the wrong amount of air
2. Pushing of the air
3. Running out of breath too quickly
4. Tension in the breath
5. Poor posture

APPOGGIO

Singing does not use the same breath pattern as in normal speech. It requires a higher rate of breath energy to maintain a sufficiently energized vocal line. Although this energy can be explained in technical terms, the more natural use of intent and attitude works best (as explained in Chapter One).

Appoggio (*Italian,* leaning into) is produced when the singer maintains a high sternum and expanded rib cage posture used in a deep inhalation. If the rib cage collapses while releasing air, it will allow the diaphragm to descend rapidly, causing the singer to lose support and run out of breath. So, keeping a high sternum and expanded rib cage through the whole process will help maintain breath integrity and support and keep the throat open, allowing for a relaxed vibrato and fuller resonance.

When working correctly, *appoggio* helps the singer maintain a longer and more stable air supply, enhances agility, allows an easier execution of large leaps, and helps the control of dynamics and accuracy. In conjunction with a balanced release of air through the glottis, *appoggio* is an essential vocal technique that's to be perfected before any difficult repertoire can be attempted. Here are four *appoggio* exercises that help with balancing the release of air and building strength in the diaphragm.

Sucking through the Hand and Tending to the Arm. This is an *appoggio* technique discovered and taught by flautist Keith Underwood and shared by the late Shirlee Emmons (2010). I've found this exercise to be enormously helpful in improving tone and production of air and share an excerpt of Emmons's description of it here:

Underwood has discovered that an inhalation achieved by vigorously sucking in the air will, without fail, stimulate a maximum expansion of the ribs extending even to the back of the body. To make sure that the effort is strong enough to set up the proper rib expansion, he has devised a way to inhale: holding up the left hand in front of your face, the thumb touching the palm, the second finger vertical before your mouth, surround that knuckle with your mouth. Then, making a loud, vulgar sucking noise, pull in the air. You will immediately note that the upper torso is relaxed except for the ribs, which expand greatly.

After all these years of hearing how the back is so important, and, in many cases, being unable to a strong back expansion, you will finally feel the back fill with air. So simple, so sure a result. It is the strength of the sucking that makes the ribs respond. . . . With the inhalation being accomplished by sucking past the knuckle of your left hand in front of your face, raise your right arm straight in the air above your head. As you begin to sing, trying at the same time to keep the ribs expanded for the entire phrase, move your right arm down toward your leg. The arm must move at the same speed for the entire trip down to the leg. If you start fast, you must continue fast. If your right hand arrives at your leg early (before the phrase has finished), you must try again, until the movement coincides exactly with the phrase you are singing. The arm must not stop during the movement downward. (This generally happens when you think about some vocal technical problem.) If you move the right arm too slowly, and do not arrive at the leg until after the phrase has finished, you must try again. The faults in the descent of the arm demonstrate that you have been using too much air or too little air or stopping your air in various places. When the arm arrives at the leg exactly at the end of the last note, having made the entire trip at the same speed, your singing will have improved immensely—musically and vocally—and appear to possess more air than ever before.

The Straw Technique. The great vocal pedagogue Ingo Titze has developed a technique that not only connects the breath, but is truly remarkable in helping free throat strain by stretching and relaxing the vocal folds and narrowing the vocal tract to help relieve the effort at the vocal folds. After working with a straw two to five minutes twice a day, one will notice that the placement of the voice is higher and buzzier in the face.

Using a fairly thin straw, place it between the lips and start to blow while phonating on a glide from as low to as high as possible. Choir directors often call this gliding "sirens." Don't let any air escape out the nostrils or sides of the mouth around the straw and be sure to use a lot of abominable muscle support to keep the tone steady. Also, when accenting a note, making a leap, or gliding up to a higher note in this exercise, be sure to use a belly accent and not a throat accent by kicking out with the belly to make the leap instead of jumping up into the throat. Notice that this is the same support you are looking for when using the *appoggio* technique.

The Beach Ball. Do you remember how great it felt to go swimming at the local beach when you were a kid? My family used to take inflatable rafts and beach balls along, and I would often try to push the beach ball below the water and then let go and watch it shoot up into the air. Or I would try to balance on it as long I could before it would roll me over and take me under.

In this exercise I want you to remember the resistance you felt from the beach ball against your hands as you tried to push it underwater. Stand on both feet, a shoulder's width apart, and pretend you're at the beach, up to your waist in the water with a beach ball in your hands. Now take a nice low breath, then pretend to push the ball about halfway under the water as you release a nice, solid "hah" on a single note. Feel the resistance against your hands, and the tenseness in your stomach muscles as you try to maintain enough pressure to keep the ball halfway under. Notice there is not tenseness in the throat as you keep a nice solid tone going. Now let the ball up to the surface as you take a new low breath. Push the ball down again while singing the same "hah" note, but this time sing a leap of a fifth by pushing the ball a little farther under the water past the halfway mark. Feel the resistance in your hands (and gut) as you make the leap in your voice. Now do a series of glides and jumps with the voice as you repeatedly push down on the ball, the farther under the water the larger the jump or glide. Never "come off your breath" by releasing the ball to the water's surface. Maintain a solid, *appoggio* support through the entire length of phonation. When you have finished holding on to the note, release the pressure on the ball and let it pop up to the surface again. Remember what this resistance feels like and never sing without it.

The Wall Push. Put both hands on a wall at shoulder height and place your feet back about three feet. Bend one knee and lean into the wall while at the same time taking a low breath. As soon as your shoulders are close to the wall, start singing a solid "ah," then push off slowly while holding the tone (the pitch will glide up). Feel the abdominal muscles tense? While taking another low breath, lean back into the wall (like doing upright push-ups) and push off hard, this time jumping up to a higher pitch. Keep doing this while playing with glides and leaps as you push away from the wall.

"Vibration of the voice is like the string. Breath is like the bow. What is this added help? Regular vibration. Like resin, it prevents slipping." —LAMPERTI

CONNECTING THE CORDS

The ability of the vocal folds to connect (hook up) with the air flowing through the glottis determines air effectiveness, ease of singing, and strength of tone. Having worked with hundreds of high school students, I've found an important need to help these students find where and how a solid onset begins. Many young students, especially those who sing in choirs, have an airy, wispy tone indicating a lack of strong connection with the vocal folds. Many others have a stuck or muffled sound, indicating a lack of pure vowels and misplaced tongue. Both problems keep the singer from acquiring an acoustically clear and ringing tone. Here are a few exercises to clear up that airy tone.

Using the Stage Voice. Pretend you're onstage and a guy with a mustache is sitting in the back row of the theater. You have something important to say to him, so to make sure he hears you clearly you take a quick, deep, low breath, and speak as loudly as possible without yelling. Let's try something like, "Hi! What are you doing back there? The theater isn't open yet!" Keep an open throat, speak connected and legato, and energetically enunciate the words to make sure you're heard. Be conscious of how the words and sound feel in the mouth (placed in the lips), throat (open and relaxed), and lower diaphragm (contracted and tight). This is the same energetic intent, support, and mouth position that you need when you're singing. In fact, speaking the text of your song in this type of energized stage voice is very helpful preliminary work before learning your music.

The Creaking Door. This exercise teaches the beginning singer to connect to their vocal folds in a much more efficient manner using imitation. We've all heard a creaking door in a scary movie that creates an eerie sound by increasing from slower to faster creaks. In this exercise we try to imitate the sound using vocal fry slowly at first, then creaking faster until reaching a solid tone. I've found this very helpful, especially with young women who have a wispy choral sound. Since they've never really connected with their vocal cords while singing, a sizable amount of air escapes through the folds, creating an airy sound. By first starting with the vocal fry creak and moving into a solid tone, the student feels exactly where the cords are attaching at the glottis. After just a short time of this exercise the student can then try singing a strong onset without the fry part anymore and will feel a huge difference in strength of tone.

The Monkey/The Insect. By using pure vowels to produce a forward, in-the-mask position (*squillo*), this exercise helps reduce the pressure on the vocal folds, which are most likely causing an overly dark sound in the voice, and allow the singer to efficiently produce more sound with less effort. Similar to the twang created in *voce di strega* (*Italian*, voice of the witch), this exercise also creates higher formant frequencies and assists with vocal fold closure.

In this exercise we want to imitate a monkey by sounding the vowel "ee" in staccatoed succession. Tenseness in the abdominal muscles should be present throughout this entire exercise (*appoggio*). After taking a small breath, hold the vocal folds closed like you do before you say the word "ow" (after stubbing your toe). Start the "ee" sound exactly from that same glottal spot (with the tip of the tongue against the bottom teeth), producing the sound as much in the teeth as possible, with no open-throated help and no breath. Cut off the sound immediately with the same glottal pressure and repeat.

Remember, the vowel must be as pure as possible, with no hint of "ih" in it. Once the Monkey exercise is mastered, we take this unfinished product and start filling out the resonance behind the vowel by engaging the lips in the "oo" position (sounds like a German umlauted u, "ü"). This lifts the soft palate and lowers the larynx enough to open the throat and allow the formant tuning needed for the optimal acoustical space in the vocal tract.

"The Insect" is an extension of "The Monkey." Start the pure "ee" on as high a pitch as possible (falsetto range for guys) and hold it. Vary the pitch and pretend there is an insect flying around the room. You can monitor the purity of the vowel placement by the size of the insect. The best result is if it sounds like a mosquito. A fly is pretty good, too. But if it sounds like a big fat bumblebee, the vowel placement has fallen too far back in the mouth and the purity of the vowel is compromised (too much "ih").

The singer will notice that they use very little air, have the ability to "ride" and "bounce" on the air, and easily crescendo and decrescendo when in the position of the mosquito. While keeping this bright, forward position (chiaro), the singer is able to apply more low support while opening the throat (adding the oscuro) and vary the dynamics from *ppp* to *fff* and back, not with more and less breath, but by altering the space in the vocal tract (formant tuning). However, the farther the vowel is out of position (fat bumblebee and larger), the more the singer starts pushing, losing the ability for dynamic control. To maintain balance of breath throughout an entire song, all phrases must start in this small "monkey" or "mosquito" position, immediately followed by an opening of the throat (go to the "oo" lips position) to add resonance, all without losing the pure forward placement of the vowel.

In short, the classical/opera singer, after finding the connected vocal cord onset, immediately opens up the vocal tract (this includes releasing the false vocal cords) into a large, resonant space while maintaining the forward placement of the pure vowel, producing the required harmonics for a large, resonant voice, allowing the performer to sing without a microphone. But how can this technique be used while singing other musical styles?

BEL CANTO'S RELATIONSHIP TO CCM VOCAL TECHNIQUE

Contemporary Commercial Music (CCM) styles such as pop, R&B, country, musical theater, rock, jazz, and folk can use my "Monkey/Mosquito" exercise to find the same onset of the vocal folds and vowel placement used in classical singing. The difference is that, although the frontal placement is important for all styles, with contemporary music there's not as much need for the large resonant space used by opera singers. By keeping the pressure off the vocal folds and primarily in the forward *voce di strega*, or chiaro position, the musical theater singer finds it much easier to belt, the rock singer to yell correctly, the R&B and jazz singer to sing high into their falsetto range, and all of them to have amazing dynamics on a microphone.

Meanwhile. . . in the larynx: For CCM style, when belting and singing in the falsetto range, the singer uses the two laryngeal muscle groups in coordination. The upper cricothyroid muscles "mix" with the lower thyroarytenoid muscles all the way up to their highest notes. The singer avoids a "break" through the *passaggio* and a "reaching" for the high notes by keeping the cords in the same position as when one speaks. This is different than the classical singer's "mix," where the upper cricothyroid muscles take over much of the work from the lower thyroarytenoid muscles in the *passaggio*, thus creating two registers (chest and falsetto for men, and chest and head voice for women).

CCM singing is almost always related to Speech Level Singing (SLS), used by many of the "Teacher to the Stars" teacher types online. This is a style developed by Seth Riggs, who actually started his career in in New York with opera and on Broadway, and then moved out to California, where he has taught hundreds of the top R&B, rock, and pop singers in the world. In my "Resources for Singers" section in Appendix II, I've included online sources for voice teachers who teach contemporary styles, those teachers who have a lot of performance experience and a foundation in *bel canto* technique in their own training. Young singers have to be so careful in their choice of teachers, especially those supposedly teaching contemporary technique, because many are undertrained. It's basically the Wild West out there with hundreds of teachers who take shortcuts with their students, boast that they're the best, say they offer something new only they can teach, and want a ton of money for it. For those singers looking to sing in contemporary styles, I encourage many hours of research before starting with a new teacher, and above all don't try learning with a CD or online course. Only a highly trained teacher who teaches in person (or at least online) can correct your every mistake in real time. Only through modification of mistakes can a singer find the experience it takes to sing correctly. Chapter Six offers a detailed guide to finding a voice teacher.

Teachers primarily teaching *bel canto* style often have new students wanting to be the next "American Idol" or equivalent, so I hope I've helped the reader see the importance of learning more about contemporary styles and shown how CCM and *bel canto* have some commonality in the way registers are mixed. I know many classical teachers look down on and are stubborn about learning about CCM, but if they want a full private studio, they will have to know some of the contemporary techniques and exercises used. I won't discuss CCM further in this book, but the online sources in Appendix II will give you much to look at.

MESSA DI VOCE

Because of the breath and laryngeal control it takes, *messa di voce* (*Italian*, to put forth, or bud) is one of the most difficult vocal effects to master as a singer. This gradual swelling and diminishing on a single tone is also "one of the most essential to master in order for the singer to be as musical and expressive as possible" (Reid, 1950), and can be used as a pedagogical tool to help join vocal registers.

The ability to crescendo to *fortissimo* and back to *pianissimo* on a long note or phrase indicates that the singer has mastered laryngeal control such as we used in the earlier Monkey/Insect exercise, and along with coordinated breath, pitch, compression, larynx, and resonance control used when singing *sotto voce* (as explained in Chapter Two).

USE OF INFLECTIONS AND GLIDES

The inflection and the glide should be approached vocally in the same way. I often work with students who can talk with large glides in their spoken inflections (Example: when saying "What?"), but when asked to sing a glide between two pitches can only jump or jog their voice from one note to another. They sometimes get embarrassed, because when asked to do an inflection again, there's no problem. The introduction of two specific pitches throws them off, and when played by a percussive instrument like a piano they often try to (subconsciously) imitate the piano and can't imagine in their heads the glide between the two notes.

Once the student has gone back and forth between inflection and the glide, the muscles in their throat start to recognize that they are basically the same action, with the difference being the glide is more supported and open throated. Once a solid glide is established it's a matter of balancing the breath support and establishing the ideal spacing in the throat and mouth as the voice ascends and descends.

When ascending, the throat naturally wants to start clamping up and choke off the highest notes. There are three ways to fix this natural reflex:

1. Always think forward no matter whether ascending or descending. The hills and valleys of a vocalise or song should not be approached as up or down, but always forward. I talk about how to practice this in the next section.
2. This fix is my favorite and should be mastered before graduating to forward movement as explained in number one: The singer has to counteract the natural clamping reflex of the throat when singing high notes by thinking down into their support as the notes ascend. The higher the note, the lower the support. A leap of a fifth means supporting a fifth down; a leap of an octave means opening the throat and supporting that high note with a low breath support an octave lower. Glides and arpeggios are practiced slowly until the lowering of the support corresponds directly with the speed and width of the ascending line. Repeating this action over and over again builds the muscles in the diaphragm and will easily add a major third onto the upper range, if not more.
3. In the matter of vocal leaps, imagine a trapdoor dropping out below you when jumping to a higher note. Or, if you are going up a scale or glide, imagine two pillars in your throat that widen as your voice ascends higher and higher. *Exercise:* Put your hands in front of you as if praying. These are the two pillars. As you ascend on the glide feel the stretch in the throat as you pull your hands apart, all while maintaining forward vowel placement.

Pointing down and forward with the hand as you're going up will remind you to think down into your lower breath support as you approach your upper range. Be careful, however; even though the vowel wants to modify on its own, the higher the notes the more exacting the singer has to be by maintaining forward vowel placement for correct airflow and to keep the vowels from spreading and falling back into the mouth. What helps for me is to always imagine the placement of sound an inch in front of the mouth.

LINE

As the singing voice is considered a natural extension of the speaking voice, much is to be gained by using the natural inflections and emotional range used in everyday speech. With a glide the singer should consider the connection between two notes in the same fashion as an inflection. If the student has trouble singing glides, they will also have problems connecting their text and making interval leaps in a legato style. Here are some exercises to correct this problem.

Glide and Inflection. Start low on the word "What?" and raise the pitch as one would when asking a question. Once that feeling is in the voice, sing a fifth on an "ah" glide. Feel that? The connection and vocal ease of the glide should be as free as the inflection. In fact, it's the same process. If the glide between the two notes isn't free, go back and feel the spoken inflection again. Continue going back and forth between the glide and inflection until it feels exactly the same. Now connect the notes in the same fashion, only this time think down into the low breath support and forward while ascending to the fifth. This keeps the throat open and stops it from closing and "reaching" for the top note. Now, when approaching the fifth there must be no hesitation of the forward movement or a relaxing of the breath support.

One of the biggest mistakes that even established singers make is to relax the support after reaching the high note and before resuming the down glide. Yes, it's a natural thing for the singer to feel they've accomplished hitting the high note, so why not relax and let gravity take the glide down? But that's a big mistake, as it's not the high note that is the most important in the phrase; it's the last note. Relaxing the support after reaching the top causes airflow to slow down against the vocal folds, which either stops phonation, causes the voice to "crack," or automatically places the support in a higher and more pushed position, weakening the core sound on the descending glide. While singing text this may also affect vowel placement and pitch.

So, in a circle pattern, once the glide has reached its high point (in this case the fifth), continue the low support forward while descending to the tonic. One should start this circle slowly at first in order to find an even connection through the whole range of the circle. Once everything is connecting well, speed up the circle. Notice that the connection has eliminated any manipulation of notes with the throat. When perfectly balanced there is not a feeling of up and down, only forward. Remember, notes are produced with lower breath support and a good ear for pitch, never with manipulation of the throat.

The Lasso. To create "line" in the voice and make this connection, I often have the student pretend they're swinging a lasso by rotating their hand in the air while singing glides (inflections) up and down on a vowel, imitating large circles for large intervals and smaller circles for small intervals.

The Crystal Glass. Another way to achieve the same line is to have the student hold a glass or soda can, or just shape their thumb and index finger of their left hand into an O, and then use the index finger of the right hand to draw a circle around the rim. Imitate the pressure and speed it takes to make a crystal glass ring while at the same time making a circle with a voice inflection. Make sure you don't skip through the glide and keep thinking forward through the tone.

FORWARD MOVEMENT

Slowing down or stopping the forward movement of breath at any time causes the low breath support to jump up to the chest or neck, causing that strained, pushed sound we are trying to avoid, and the loss of air needed to get through the musical note or phrase. It is not a natural act to sustain and excite the breath needed to sing with a strong tone, and mastering it takes years of conscious effort and practice.

Keeping the breath support solid and continuous is essential if one is to continue to the end of a phrase without running out of air. I've just explained the importance of the correct connection to the sound and falling into the breath. Once the tone is established, it is now important to sustain the support needed to sing to the end of the phrase. This takes intent (see more on intent in Chapter Four) and an energized breath stream riding a balanced air supply through a pure placement of vowels. There are a number of different visualizations and exercises I do to maintain this support:

> **Walking the Table.** While performing this exercise, always be conscious of the breath coming from your lower support while keeping a loose jaw and open throat. Sing a phrase from a song or a vocalise while walking along the side of a table (or piano or edge of something at waist height) with your finger pushing forward along the edge. Support the phrase with your finger to the end of the table as you sing the phrase. If there's a leap or gradual ascension in the music, walk even faster, pushing the finger forward to support the energy needed to get up to that note. This is really when the *appoggio* kicks in.

As I've mentioned earlier, when you've reached the top note and are about to descend, keep the support moving forward like you're still ascending. Don't hesitate or pull back at all after you hit that top note. Continue moving forward and then maintain that energy to the end of the phrase. This is a major problem even for well-trained singers. They mistakenly think that just because they've sung the high note they can relax and let gravity take them down to the end of the phrase. It's a natural reflex, but a big mistake. The instant the singer hesitates or releases the forward moving support, the throat and vowels collapse, and the singer runs out of air. Remember, the last note is the most important note in the phrase, not the high note!

Walking the Room. Like walking the table, start taking small steps, walking slowly forward with intent (like a cat about to attack) while singing the phrase (without pushing your finger along a surface). As the notes ascend or the notes become melismatic, start moving fast and even leap forward if there is a big leap in the music. Once the climax in the phrase has been reached, do not slow down, but continue to move forward to the end of the phrase.

In this chapter I've explained many aspects of how to energize, balance, and strengthen the breath. Through these exercises we've generally used vowels and speech. However, the art of singing requires the student to master the ability to not only breathe life into the tone, but also to be understood while infusing and interpreting the emotion and meaning behind the text. In our next chapter we'll be covering all the aspects needed to make that happen.

FOUR

The Language Connection

"The power to group words and phrases of a song together making one continuous whole stamps the real singer."
—LAMPERTI

CONNECTING THE VOICE TO TEXT

Singing masterfully requires a complete comprehension of the text. Our ultimate goal as singing artists is to communicate attitude, inflection, texture, confidence, inspiration, insights, feelings, and instincts to our audience to the best of our capabilities.

I believe that to achieve artistry, the singer should have three objectives when choosing text for repertoire that is technically appropriate for them. They should look for texts that:

1. Have something beautiful to say. Repertoire that uses beauty as a major theme is descriptive and often spiritually inspired or describes nature.
2. Reflect their age or life experience. Repertoire that matches the singer's emotional maturity.
3. Have something relevant to say, according to the singer's life perspective.

As singers we can look at ourselves as messengers, using vibration as a delivery system in the shape of musical text. Only by mastering our technical skills to the highest level, while using the imaginative vehicle of text to create beautiful messages, can this delivery system achieve artistry at the highest level.

> "Never pull the voice away from its focus, nor push the breath up from its foundation, nor let diction leave the lips." —LAMPERTI

WHY DOES SHE/HE SING SO STRANGELY?

How often have you listened to an inexperienced classical singer (and many experienced ones) and were unable to understand what language he/she was singing? Just the opposite, how many times have you heard a popular country ballad on the radio and were able to understand every word with no problem? Why is that? Why do we understand the country singer so much more than the classical singer if they're both singing English? Also, what happens when a classical singer is perfectly understood when they're speaking to the audience and introducing their song, and then loses the ability to be understood when they start to sing?

It's something I call "singer mode." The student's face may be perfectly at ease when they announce their piece, but when taking their first breath to sing the eyebrows go up, the forehead wrinkles, and the face contorts into a completely unnatural position. They're getting ready to "sing." The sound comes out unbalanced and either sounds pushed, too bright, or feels and sounds like a lot of work. That's because it usually is. All of a sudden there's tension in the face and neck, they're breathing from the chest, and everything is pushed. What's up with that?

Sure, nerves have a lot to do with it, but I've found that many young singers taking their first private voice lesson have developed bad habits from choral singing. It could be the result of trying to blend with the rest of the choir by pulling the vowels back into their mouth, so their voice won't "stick out." The choir director may have asked them not to use vibrato, wanting everyone to sing straight tone. They may have been asked to sing alto when they were really a soprano (they were short on altos that year) or sing tenor when they were really a baritone. Any of these things could contribute to a bad vocal habit or tension in the body, but predominantly in the face, neck, and shoulders.

In this chapter we'll look at how to deliver sung text in a balanced, tension-free manner using basic principles of speech as a foundation.

"The difference between speaking and singing is continuity of vibration and energy. In speaking, momentum is constantly arrested; in singing, never." —LAMPERTI

SPEECH vs. SINGING

Good speech can be considered the foundation of good singing. To sing well, the basic principles of speech must be in place. These principles include line, projection, posture, breathing, and articulation. But speech differs from the singing voice in several ways, including:

1. Speech isn't tied to tonal intervals (the range in speech being much shorter).
2. Fewer formants are used in speech (F0, F1, F2), while singing incorporates more partials and overtones above the lower fundamental tones (F3, F4, F5).
3. Speech isn't sustained, while song is.

> *"Words are but dyes that tint the focused vibration of the voice with their colors."* —LAMPERTI

PROJECTION

When singing, the distribution of sound energy is significantly higher than in speech. In other words, singing has more intensity than speech. This is accomplished by thinking forward through the phrase, keeping the vowels as pure or as much like properly enunciated speech as possible, and extending that support throughout the entire range of the voice.

In sung vowels the formants (see Chapter Three) tend to be approximately ten decibels louder than the formants in speech. This is mostly because of the lack of the reinforcing upper three quality formants (F_3 thru F_5) used by singers. These singer's formants, used to reinforce and thus amplify the fundamental frequency, are rarely used in speech.

Building a bridge between regular speech and the use of singer's formants can be realized using a four-step process.

1. Choose a phrase from a song and speak it as you would normally.
2. Using the same phrase, pretend you're onstage and talking to an imaginary gentleman in the back row of the theater. Take a low breath and project the phrase with a supported stage voice, like you mean it. Notice what's happening with your body. You're enunciating the words more than usual (which keeps your lips engaged and in a fluted position) and your diaphragm is tight with the support you're using to project your sound.

3. Now, with the same support and energy, sing the same phrase on one pitch, making sure you're doing everything you did in #2. All words should be connecting legato style using the 95 percent vowel, 5 percent consonant formula described earlier.
4. Finally, either making up a melody or using the music that contains the text, sing the phrase. By using all the elements in this process (along with a relaxed throat) the phrase should have a well-supported tone and be understood by every listener.

PRELIMINARY TEXT PREPARATION

Preparing the text of a song or aria correctly involves a systematic and coordinated effort between rhythm, correct pronunciation of the language being sung, and consistent breath support to project the sound to the audience. The student may have their vocalises and scales down pat, but unless those vowels stay pure and open and consonants are lined up and rhythmically correct with actual words, there is a lot that can go wrong. So, unless the student's language and sight-reading skills are excellent, I suggest they familiarize themselves with the language being sung and then learn their music in stages.

SINGING IN A FOREIGN LANGUAGE

Young classical singers traditionally work on songs in their native language first because they can more easily control its inflections (a very important tool for expression) and can use their tongue and lips in a standard manner. They then repeatedly recite the texts with as much phonetical accuracy as possible so there is no tripping over words before attempting to sing the piece. However, the fundamental principles of phonetics and speech in a foreign language must be seriously studied before attempting to sing a foreign text. Because of the open vowels, Italian is almost always the first foreign language an English-speaking classical singer studies, followed by German and then French. It is now becoming much more common to also study Spanish, Russian, Swedish, and Czech. But if you are a singer studying voice in the American university system, Italian, German, and French are the foreign languages most commonly taught.

The ideal way to study another language is to travel to that country and immerse yourself in the language and culture. Nothing ignites the imprinting of a new language in one's head, ear, and tongue better than to be thrown headfirst into a country where the language is predominant. Europeans have an advantage over Americans because of the close proximity of countries with these other languages, but there are still many ways Americans and Canadians can learn languages if they don't have the luxury of spending a great deal of time abroad.

Singing a language offers more challenges than just learning how to speak the language. Here are different ways to learn Italian, German, and French if you are not lucky enough to live in those countries for a time:

> **Conservatory or University Training.** Although language requirements differ from school to school, the basic language courses required of an undergraduate bachelor of music or bachelor of fine arts student majoring in voice performance include at least one year of basic English, Italian, German, and French plus one semester of English, Italian, German, and French diction (with the use of IPA, the International Phonetic Alphabet). If the student decides to continue with their schooling and earn a master's or doctorate degree in voice performance, they will need to take more language courses.
>
> While students are taking these language courses they are, of course, being taught to use foreign languages in songs

and arias by their voice teacher and coaches. Students typically have a weekly one-hour voice lesson and sing in ensembles such as choir and opera workshop that perform repertoire in foreign languages. Some schools may differ, but as a voice professor I usually found that freshman voice students learn English and Italian songs and arias, then add German in their sophomore year and French the following year. Depending on the voice teacher, a Spanish, Latin, Swedish/Norwegian/Danish, Russian, Czech, or Asian piece may also occasionally be included in the student's repertoire.

Private Coaching. If you prefer to study classical voice independently and can afford more than a private voice teacher, hiring a coach and language tutor is important. Try to find people prolific in both speaking and singing the foreign language (ask the local university voice department or opera company for teachers and coaches in the area). Students can also find online courses that offer one-on-one tutoring sessions and language immersion courses to learn the language (more info on these resources is in Appendix II).

Immersion Course. Personally, I prefer taking a course in the country where the language is spoken. There are many in Italy, Germany, and France specializing in teaching English speakers their language. However, if the time requirement or expense rules out this option, students can find foreign language immersion courses in the larger cities. For example, "Alliance Française" is a language school that teaches French immersion and has chapters in many of the bigger cities in the United States. Once a student completes the course, he or she should hire a singing coach to incorporate the language with the singing voice.

Home and Internet Language Courses. There are many language courses and apps meant to be used at home to learn a language at your leisure. I list a number of these in Appendix II, but some of my favorites include Rosetta Stone, Rocket Language, and Babbel.

INTERNATIONAL PHONETIC ALPHABET (IPA)

To be phonetically accurate in the pronunciation of any singing language, taking a course in IPA (International Phonetic Alphabet) is highly recommended for the singing student and is always required of voice majors in a college or university. Although IPA is used extensively to teach the pronunciation of the spoken word, we will only be dealing with its singing application here.

Developed in 1886 by the International Phonetic Association, IPA is based on the Latin alphabet and uses 107 letters, 52 diacritics (glyphs or marks added on or around a letter), and four prosodic marks (representing the rhythm or stress of the word). No matter what country you are from or what kind of dialect you use, IPA is the great equalizer, using symbols to represent each distinct sound made (or pronunciation) in the spoken or sung language. Although different languages use different sounds (such as accents, colloquialisms, nasality, or inflections), most of the vowels and consonants are the same and can be used to transcribe words in French, German, Spanish, English, Latin, and Italian, for example—all in accurate, one symbol-per-sound communication. The following chart shows the English IPA vowel and consonant symbols.

IPA Symbols in General American Dialect

The Cardinal vowel system, as shown below, is used to describe the height, backness, and roundness of the IPA vowel sounds and was developed by Daniel Jones, a phonetician in the early twentieth century.

THE INTERNATIONAL PHONETIC ALPHABET (IPA)

FORWARD VOWELS

SYMBOL	SOUNDS LIKE
[i]	m*ee*t
[ɪ]	m*i*t
[e]	m*a*ke
[ɛ]	m*e*t
[æ]	m*a*t
[a]	m*i*te

CENTRAL VOWELS

SYMBOL	SOUNDS LIKE
[ʌ]	sh*u*t (stressed *uh*)
[ə]	*a*round (unstressed *uh*)
[ɜ]	w*or*d (r-sounding vowel, stressed)
[ɚ]	weath*er* (r-sounding vowel, unstressed)

BACK VOWELS

SYMBOL	SOUNDS LIKE
[u]	sh*oo*t
[ʊ]	sh*oo*k
[o]	s*o*, s*ew*
[ɔ]	s*aw*
[ɑ]	sh*o*t

DIPTHONGS

SYMBOL	SOUNDS LIKE
[eɪ]	b*ai*t
[oʊ]	c*oa*t
[aɪ]	k*i*te
[aʊ]	h*ow*
[ɔɪ]	t*oy*
[ju]	*u*sually

CONSONANTS

SYMBOL	SOUNDS LIKE
[b]	*b*ear
[ç]	*h*ue
[tʃ]	*ch*urch
[ts]	bi*ts*
[d]	*d*og
[dʒ]	*J*ordan
[f]	*f*ood
[g]	*g*oat
[h]	*h*ate
[hw]	*wh*ere
[x]	Ba*ch*
[j]	*y*ellow
[k]	*k*itchen
[kw]	*qu*ickly
[l]	*l*ong
[m]	*m*ight

SYMBOL	SOUNDS LIKE
[n]	*n*o
[ɲ]	u*ni*on
[ŋ]	si*ng*
[p]	*p*ain
[r]	*r*ate
[ɾ]	spa*rr*ow
[s]	*s*ay
[ʃ]	*sh*oot
[t]	*t*oday
[θ]	*th*ick
[ð]	*th*at
[v]	*v*iper
[w]	*w*e
[z]	*z*oo
[ʒ]	we*dg*y

If you haven't studied IPA you may want to have a native-speaking friend record the text for you or listen to a famous singer sing it first before you work on it. Your voice teacher will probably go through the pronunciation with you, but hiring a language coach who works with singers is the best route.

Some song anthologies, vocal pedagogy texts, and reference works such as *Phonetic Readings of Songs and Arias* by Coffin, Errolle, Singer and DeLattre (1994) contain dependable transcriptions of foreign language songs. Two other references in the learning of IPA include *International Phonetic Alphabet for Singers: A Manual for English and Foreign Language Diction* by Joan Wall (1989), and *The Structure of Singing* (1986), by Richard Miller.

DICTION

The critical aspect of diction is often minimized by teachers of singing. Ignoring diction compromises and impedes the student from understanding the importance of established aspects of diction used in all languages and styles. These include text, balance of air, correct phrasing, dynamic energy, expressive diction (enunciation), correct dynamics, and word stress. Moving along from IPA, below you will find other aspects of diction that are equally as important.

VOWELS

Vowels are sounds produced and expanded in an open position in the vocal tract as the central part of a given syllable and are essential in creating sound quality. In fact, producing pure vowels in an open position, the most important component of an effective acoustical space, creates and defines the tone and helps to make text more understandable to the listener.

Spoken vowels are usually identified by one high and one low formant (F1 and F2), which are produced by two resonators, the pharyngeal (throat) and coupled oral resonator (mouth). The F1 formant corresponds to the opened and closed vowels, while the F2 formant is produced by a backward and forward positioning of the vowel placement. The continuous transition from extreme open/front vowels such as "ee" to closed/back vowels such as "oo" in normal speech patterns makes use of the jaw opening, tongue constriction, and an increase in lip-rounding that is needed to produce enhanced F1 and F2 formant harmonics.

As explained in Chapter Two, while F1 and F2 formants are used for speaking, F3, F4, and F5 are the formants used in singing, which when combined create the "singer's formant," or ring in the voice (*squillo*). Pure vowels are necessary for achieving this ring and defining the timbre characteristics of the sound. Open vowels prolong resonance using the nasal, oral, and labial cavities and shape the vocal tract primarily with the lips and tongue in a vertical movement. On the contrary, the use of horizontal, or side-to-side movement of the mouth while articulating words, tends to spread the forward vowels and contribute to the loss of good tone quality (i.e., quality formants). So, the trick is to keep the open space naturally used in back vowels while singing the forward vowels. This is done with an equalizing placement of the "oo" lips, as I've explained throughout this book. The following exercise helps the singer find the optimal space and shape needed to produce open vowels.

Working Just the Vowels

In this exercise you eliminate all of the consonants in the text and speak/sing the vowels of the text in order. Do this first on steady quarter notes and then in the song's correct rhythm, all while in a connected legato fashion. Purity of vowels and the "oo"-shaped lip position is essential (never pull back and "spread" the lips on certain vowels). Since we have not all learned IPA, I will be spelling out the vowels phonetically.

In Italian, "Sebben crudele, mi fai lanquir" is spoken "e eh oo eh eh, ee ahee ah ooee." This technique is effective for all languages, including English. Example: "The Sun whose Rays are all Ablaze" would be practiced as "uh uh oo e ah aw ah e." This exercise should be used when first working the text and later when you're singing pitches. It should be done slowly, in a connected, legato fashion. The connection of words and constant placement of vowels you achieve during this exercise is one of the most beneficial I have found in mastering airflow and a solid, consistent vocal resonance.

Modified Vowels

Modifying the acoustics of a vowel is often done intentionally by the singer, especially in the upper range of the voice. With a slight adjustment and articulation of the vowel, using the lips and tongue, it is possible to find a more pleasing tone when singing the higher notes. Though this may affect the ability to be clearly understood, it is necessary to maintain consistent space and resonance.

CONSONANTS

The expression and meaning of language are clarified by the information that consonants carry. And although their use in singing accounts for only about 5 percent of the sound heard (mostly used in starting and ending syllables), singing consonants correctly is vitally important for diction and voice projection.

All twenty-one English consonants are formed with the articulators of the mouth, which include the lips, tongue, jaw, cheeks, hard and soft palates, alveolar ridge (raised ridge behind the upper teeth), and teeth. They can be classified into three categories:

1. Closing (b, d, g, p, t, k)
2. Diverting (n, m)
3. Constricting (f, s, v, z)

Gregg (1991) summarizes that these consonants can be more accurately defined as "simple muscle contractions which in some fashion momentarily occlude the vocal tract, giving distinct sounds, which form the boundaries of vowel sounds, turning them into words."

The manner of articulation and the use of voiced and unvoiced consonants will be discussed in the section that follows.

Low vs. High Consonants

Good technique dictates that, using a relaxed jaw and open throat, the first consonant and vowel positions of the very start of a phrase must be low in order to establish and maintain a warm and round tone throughout the phrase. This means that the consonant starting the first word of the phrase starts as a double consonant (see next section) and in a low position. Example: Use the low "s" (found in the first consonant of the name "Susie") instead of the high "s" (in the first consonant of the name "Sissy") as a doubled consonant before starting a low vowel squarely on the first beat of the first word. This sets the tonal position for the entire following phrase, that is, if the singer does not lift the jaw and come out of position. This process of sounding the low consonant first, explained in the following paragraphs, should be done in metric time with the first vowel, giving the phrase a running and solid start.

Unwritten Double Consonants at the Beginning of the Phrase

While living in New York City in the 1990s I often coached repertoire with Marcello Garofalo, a master teacher of *bel canto* style, and son of Carlo Giorgio Garofalo (1886–1962), a renowned composer and opera coach for many great Italian singers, including Titta Ruffo and Beniamino Gigli. Although Maestro Garofalo's accent was thick (I'm sure I missed some important information), one thing that I have always found tremendously helpful was his emphasis on the importance of doubling consonants at the beginning of a phrase, and when needed within the line.

Doubling the first consonant in the first word of a phrase provides the energy and movement of air needed to sustain and support the upcoming phrase Although this isn't recommended in a choral situation (unless done in unison), the energy and movement of air created by a double consonant is important in singing solo repertoire. Soft consonants such as s, sh, m, n, l, w, f, and v are the easiest to produce, with hard consonants k, t, and p taking longer to learn (phrases starting with vowels deal with a different type of onset).

Exercise: Using the word "Sunday" in 4/4 time, inhale on the 1st beat, release a low "ss" on the 2nd beat, fall on the "uh" on the 3rd beat, and put "nday" on the 4th beat.
(1) Inhale, (2) SSS, (3) uuh, (4) nday

There are three very important reasons to use double consonants at the beginning of a phrase.

1. To release sub-glottal (below the vocal cords) air pressure so the air starts to move. This release of pressure equalizes the sub-glottal air with the air above the glottis and helps keep the consonants and vowels low and the throat relaxed and open through the phrase.
2. To ensure forward movement of air, followed by a pure vowel on the beat, it supports and sustains the phrase that follows. This is often called "falling into the breath."
3. For better diction. You will always understand that first word if the consonant is doubled.

Here's one of my exercises that helps develop the beginning double consonant. It's best to first practice it in rhythm while speaking. Remember, first take a low, quick breath, then sound the double consonant a half beat before placing the "ooee" on the first beat. Once you have spoken it in rhythm you then can practice it on the 5 descending steps.

Pitches:		5	4	3	2	1
(Inhale)	ll	ooee . . .	ooee . . .	ooee . . .	ooee . . .	ooee
(up ½ step)		5	4	3	2	1
(Inhale)	ll	ooee . . .	ooee . . .	ooee . . .	ooee . . .	ooee

Pitches:		5	4	3	2	1
(Inhale)	mm	ooee . . .	ooee . . .	ooee . . .	ooee . . .	ooee
(up ½ step)		5	4	3	2	1
(Inhale)	mm	ooee . . .	ooee . . .	ooee . . .	ooee . . .	ooee

Pitches:		5	4	3	2	1
(Inhale)	ssh	ooee . . .	ooee . . .	ooee . . .	ooee . . .	ooee
(up ½ step)		5	4	3	2	1
(Inhale)	ssh	ooee . . .	ooee . . .	ooee . . .	ooee . . .	ooee

Unwritten Double Consonants with the Phrase

Certain words can also be emphasized with the use of a double consonant: (Example: I llove you.) Stressing the beginning of a word anchors and solidifies the tone and keeps air from escaping too fast. It also stresses important adjectives, nouns, and action verbs in the text, which helps keep a consistently solid tone.

Leaping to a Higher Pitch

Using double consonants keeps the singer from tightening up, shoving, reaching, or hiking the voice when making a leap to a higher pitch. For example, in an exercise where you jump up an octave in the phrase "the sun," (Step 1) you would first sing the word "the" on the low note. Then, staying on the low note, (Step 2) you anticipate the word "sun" by sounding a double "ss" (as in Suzie, not Sissy), followed by (Step 3) immediately drop the jaw to pop the vowel open on the higher note. The air pressure built up behind the low s shoots the voice forward and up with no pushing or reaching. The same procedure works when using soft consonants like m or n. "The moon" would be sung "the mm^oon." Notice that the pressure behind the lips (on mm) is what shoots the voice up to the higher note, with no work at all. If the singer would have put the "m" on the top note there would be reaching and a complete shift of positioning throwing the whole vocal line out of whack. Remember to drop the jaw as fast as possible when opening the vowel on the top note. A slow, tight, or hesitant jaw movement will not work.

Exercise for Using Consonants Before Large Leaps

My favorite exercise to build this technique is sung on "mah" or starts with any soft consonant (Example, "sh" or "ss"), as shown on the next page. Make sure the rhythm is exact through the entire exercise.

Start with a quick and low breath, followed by a double "mm" before hitting the "ah" on the first beat, followed by the double "mm" of the second beat. This sets you up for quickly opening the mouth and shooting up to the note an octave above on the third beat. After holding the top note for two beats, without letting up on the forward movement, continue a legato arpeggio forward through the end of the exercise. Watch in the mirror to make sure the mouth does not start to close or change (don't move the jaw in time with the descending notes) when thinking forward (not down) through the arpeggio. Remember, when thinking support, the last note in the phrase is the most important, not the top note.

Double Consonants in Italian

There's a big difference between single and double consonants in Italian. Although we use unwritten double consonants to start Italian phrases, as explained in the last few pages, written double consonants are used in the middle of words such as "bella" or "mamma." In English we would pronounce these words "be-la" and "ma-ma," ending the first syllable with a vowel and beginning the second syllable with a consonant. Italians pronounce them "bel:la" or "mam:ma," ending the first syllable with a consonant as well as starting the second syllable with the same consonant.

With soft consonants such as the "l" in "bel:la" the singer must not hold on to the preceding vowel but jump into and sustain the "l" longer. With words like "mam:ma" there is a perceived stopping of sound. This should not be taken as a stop in forward movement, however, as the double "m" is pressurized in the lips, ready to slightly explode into the following "a," keeping the forward movement of the phrase intact. I visualize this as the space when a skateboarder jumps off a surface and lands onto another surface. There is no sound of the wheels during the leap in between surfaces, but that doesn't mean the skateboarder is stopping momentum before touching the next surface.

SHADOW VOWELS

Shadow vowels are unwritten yet audible (voiced) sounds in the text. They're used to clarify diction, lengthen the proceeding vowel, help with breath support and pitch, and keep the energy of the phrase moving forward. Shadow vowels can be used on appropriate words throughout a phrase as follows:

1. Before a catch breath or rest.
2. As a neutral vowel ("uh" schwa sound) between two consonants in a word. This is used extensively in English art song and especially musical theater pieces. Example: blow = buhllow, glide = guhllide, strong = sterrong.
3. On the last word of the phrase (except k, t, and p). I find that using an "ih" instead of a schwah "uh" (as most singers do) at the end of the phrase keeps the pitch up, energy moving forward, and air placement in the correct position ready for the beginning of the next phrase. Example: sound = soun(-dih), sun = suhn(nih). This high placement of the shadow vowel may seem insignificant at first, but the singer will soon find it to be an extremely helpful tool in keeping the energy moving forward, helping to maintain balanced airflow, and keeping the pitch centered and consistent.

Be careful—shadow vowels must be present but never overexaggerated! Experiment with them until they sound as natural as possible.

K, T, AND P ENDINGS

K, T, and P endings are very similar to shadow vowel endings as they also must explode from a compression of air held at the front of the mouth. These consonants are different however, as they have plosive stops and are unvoiced (a puff of air or aspiration making a brief "h" sound following the consonant). Here are a few examples. Wake = Wa(kih), late = la(tih), or whip = whi(pih). To test the unvoiced difference between shadow vowels and K, T, and P endings, put your hand or a candle in front of your mouth. You will feel it or see the flame flicker with the puff following the consonant. Similar to the shadow vowel's "ih" instead of "uh" position, keep these plosives in a high position to maintain and energize the forward movement into the next phrase.

DIPHTHONGS

Diphthongs (Greek: di, two; phthongos, sound) have two sounds on the same syllable and are produced by two movements of the articulators. It's typical that the first vowel holds on for a longer duration than the second part of the same syllable, such as in pronouncing "hi" as "haaah ee." Though English is known for this type of diphthong, different dialects in the United States often change the timing of the diphthong (Minnesotans may say "bo wuht" for boat) and often combine words, especially in the south ("yawl" instead of "you all").

One of the major problems English-speaking singers have when singing in a foreign language is their indiscriminate and inappropriate use of diphthongs. Languages such as Italian use no diphthongs (although they do use many shadow vowels), so the English-speaking singer must be extra careful to avoid them. The fastest way to eliminate unnecessary diphthongs is to monitor oneself in a mirror to see whether there is extra movement in the lips at the end of problem words.

CONNECTING SYLLABLES

To always retain a forward motion and avoid chopping up the vocal line, there has to be a constant connection between words. Except at a breath mark or rest, this "hookup" is accomplished most efficiently by attaching the ending consonant of a syllable onto the following syllable. Example: While using the 95 percent vowel and 5 percent consonant formula, connect "The sun shines clearly in the sky" in a legato fashion, like so: "The suh nshahee nsclih rlee yih nthuh skahee."

Because we don't talk like this, the concept may seem difficult at first. I find it helpful to think very legato and sometimes visualize gliding along in ice skates or spreading icing on a cake. Another way to feel connected is to smoothly walk forward as you sing. Better yet, walk forward while pushing your finger along the edge of a table or piano so you can feel the forward (see "Walking the Table" in Chapter Three) connected movement instead of just visualizing it. This develops strong breath support and keeps the phrase strong and connected as discussed in the *appoggio* technique in Chapter Three.

EXTRANEOUS VOCAL SOUNDS

Sounds not written in the music often do have an effect on the interpretation and presentation of singing text. We've already mentioned shadow vowels and diphthongs people might use in a certain dialect, but there are other sounds that can augment a singing performance if performed correctly by a trained professional. Some of those sounds include air inhalation, white noise (Example: raspiness or vocal fry from cords not connecting completely), speaking, laughs, snores, cries, whistles, snorts, belches, sneezes, catcalls, and tongue and teeth clicks.

An example of where it's used in popular music with great effect is when Michael Jackson makes extraneous cries and woops between lyrics. But in classical music it is most used by male buffo role singers, as used in some Italian comic operas, where using extraneous sounds can be very funny and can enhance the character's audience response. Using extraneous sounds for effect may come naturally to some experienced buffo singers, but often these sounds are choreographed to achieve maximum effectiveness.

SONG PREPARATION

Using a systematic approach to prepare a song is an efficient and productive way to make the most of your time. Unless the song is very simple and in your native language, this usually means working on various aspects of the song individually and later putting them together. I suggest learning a song or aria in the following order:

Musical Aspects
1. Learn the rhythm of the song by either clapping or tapping it out, first slowly, and then faster until you reach the correct tempo. Then vocalize the rhythm on a nonsense syllable such as "lah" or "dah." Using a metronome to keep and increase tempo is very helpful in this process. There are also unwritten rhythmic concerns within the text that will be explained later in this chapter.
2. Circle and underline tempo markings, dynamic markings, and melodic climaxes in pencil (not pen) in the sheet music or score.
3. Memorize the melody on a nonsense syllable like "lah" or "dah."
4. Place breath marks in music so breathing is consistent. (I often listen to at least three artists' recordings of the same piece to see where they most commonly place their breaths.)

Text
1. If the song is in a foreign language, prepare a translation for each word by placing it directly below the word being translated. Often, the music will include a transliteration of the text (a singable translation of the text). This may give the

student an idea of what they are singing about but will not be helpful in appropriately expressing the translation with the correct emphasis on key words. Although it may be faster and more convenient, I don't recommend using an online translator or foreign language app to translate the song. Going old school with a foreign language dictionary is more reliable and helps strengthen your grasp of the language. From personal experience I find that looking up words one by one in a dictionary engrains the words more firmly into the mind.
2. If the student knows IPA, they should prepare a phonetic translation. If not, they should at least note the correct sound (written in a way that will help them remember) above words they have not previously learned to pronounce.
3. Recite the text out loud until there are no diction problems. This is of the utmost importance, as cleaning up diction problems clears up a multitude of vocal problems.
4. Research the text. In other words, know the story. The more the singer can empathize with the narrative, the more expressive and musical they will be.

Coordinating Text with Rhythm

The golden rule of singing "in time" is to sound syllables squarely on the beat and place consonants and vowels exactly on their correct rhythms using the 95 percent vowel, 5 percent consonant formula noted previously. The more the text is exactly in time with the rhythm, the more solid the sound, giving the singer a sense of control and intent. Jumping in early or late on a note lessens the strength and effectiveness of the voice, often causing a weakness of support in the line.

A major problem that arises when singing text of any language, a problem that can affect many aspects of good vocal technique, is when the manipulation and coordination of the lips and tongue are out of sync with the rhythm and tempo of the music. Over-articulation (working too hard) or under-articulation (lack of exactness) of the words in relationship to the tempo of the song causes poor or inconsistent diction and creates tension in the jaw and throat, which affects resonance and vibrato. Therefore, the perfect timing and exact placement of consonants and nouns in the exact rhythm and tempo are of major importance.

Unwritten Rhythms within the Text

Properly using unwritten rhythms is a major component in differentiating good singing from excellent singing. These rhythms include:

1. The breath inhalation
2. Release of breath into the first word of the phrase, and important words in the phrase, using double consonants
3. Lengths of portamenti, mordents, trills, and other inflections
4. Rhythm of the glides, elisions, diphthongs, and triphthongs within a word
5. Shadow vowels

All of these rhythms are important in helping separate and define where the consonants and vowels of the text fall within or around a given note's time frame. And they all have to be rhythmically exact if the intent of the text is to be solid and breath support through the phrase is to be consistent.

Let's compare how unwritten rhythm is used in dance and choral conducting. Example: (1) breath inhalation, and (2) release of breath into the tone, both of which start before the first beat. A dancer leaps into the air (breath) and falls to the floor (release) before starting their dance on the beat (onset of phonation). The conductor's upbeat consists of him raising the baton (breath) and then lowering the baton (release) before hitting the first beat of the music (onset of phonation). Just as in singing, the first note or beat can't just jump out of nowhere. There has to be movement and an exactness of rhythm in this anticipation or the balance of air and breath support will be tenuous at best.

Working the Text

After forty-five years of performing and teaching, I've come to the determination that nothing is more important to cleaning up technique and fixing multiple vocal problems than working the text. Almost anything that can technically go wrong when singing can be fixed by woodshedding the diction using the techniques spoken about in this chapter. Here are a few ways to start that process:

1. Read the text as you would normally read a poem or passage from a book. At first, we don't want to work rhythmic values of the music, just the text. Let's work one phrase at a time. Although the tempo may be slow in the song, there may be places in the text that trip you up if you were to speak the phrase at a faster tempo. It doesn't matter if you can speak (or sing) the line perfectly at a slower tempo; just the inclination for a combination of words to be problematic may be inherent within the phrase. To make sure you have cleaned up even the invisible problems in your text, work through the text in the following manner.

2. Read the passage again (working two to four measures at a time), only this time read it slowly, projecting the words and supporting the sound by pretending you are talking to that guy with the mustache sitting in the back row of the theater. Your "stage voice" will keep the vowels open to their optimum duration and is exactly the same breath support you need while singing classical and musical theater pieces.

Gradually increase the speed with which you speak the line, faster and faster, to as fast as possible. Say the line or phrase fast ten times in a row (always start over if you trip over your words). If there are a few words in the phrase that get you tongue tied, just keep going over (woodshed) those words again and again (slow to fast) until your mouth, tongue, and lips are all coordinated, and the words slip out of your mouth perfectly. Once you are able to get through the language of the phrase with no trips at the fast tempo (around five times perfectly), reduce the speed to the marked tempo. You'll notice that when speaking fast, the shape of the lips has no time to fall back in the middle of words to a spread position. It is therefore much easier to retain lip and vowel placement and airflow at the slower speed.

Remember to keep your throat open and keep the energy moving forward. Again, if you are repeatedly having trouble with words in a specific spot, woodshed that sequence of words over and over, slow to fast in a legato style to smooth out the text, and then return to the full phrase you were working on.

3. Now speak the text in rhythm. Slowly at first and then speeding it up to as fast as you are able. As in the last step, when the line or phrase is mastered and you are able to repeat the text in rhythm five times in a row, reduce the speed to the marked tempo. Remember to use your "stage voice" in a legato style, making sure the syllables of the words connect by holding out the vowels as long as possible.

Working the Text from Back to Front

Although I will occasionally repeat myself in this section, the importance of clean text and its benefits to good vocal technique is most important, and the steps to learning the technique are well worth reiterating. Once there is no longer any tripping up of words, inconsistent use of vowels, or incorrect use of shadow vowels and double consonants, almost any vocal problem can be remedied.

I was singing my first Bartolo in Rossini's *The Barber of Seville* when I learned this wonderful text preparation technique from Metropolitan Opera coach and prompter Donna Racik. I've incorporated this "back to front" method in both my score study and teaching and it has served me very well through the years. While it is especially effective while working recitative, it works well when working on arias or any type of song, especially patter songs. By starting from the last word, you already have the whole line in your mouth by the time you get to the front of the sentence, compared to starting from the front, which gives you the unwanted possibility to fall apart by the end of the line. This exercise works in the following sequence:

1. Study and speak the text until feeling somewhat comfortable with it. Don't worry about the musical rhythm at this point.
2. Once the language is consistent and ironed out, speak each line of the text from back to front. Start out in a slow legato while concentrating on pronunciation.
3. Say the last two words or syllables in the line, then add the third from the last and so forth to the first word of the line. For example, here is some recitative from Mozart's opera Don Giovanni.

    Leperello: "In que-sto mon-do con-cio-sia co-sa quan-do fos-se che"

    Translation: "In this world, this is what it is like"

    Starting back to front: *fos-se che, . . . quan-do fos-se che, . . . co-sa quan-do fos-se che, . . . con-cio-sia co-sa quan-do fos-se che, . . . mon-do con-cio-sia co-sa quan-do fos-se che, In que-sto mon-do con-cio-sia co-sa quan-do fos-se che*

4. Repeat the process a little faster. If there is hesitation between any parts of the text, stop and repeat the two or three syllables that are making you tongue tied until it is smoothed out, then start from the back of the line again.
5. Repeat the process by speaking faster and faster until the text feels perfectly smooth. Be able to repeat the entire line from beginning to end perfectly at high speed at least five times in a row.
6. Sing the line.
7. First sing the recitative or song line on one pitch quickly and out of rhythm.
8. On the same pitch, slow the line down to the correct tempo and add correct rhythms and inflections.
9. Sing the melody on correct pitches and with expression.

The singer will find that after this process is done, they have not only lined up the voice with acoustical and technical efficiency, but they have also engrained the text into the memory of both the mouth and the brain.

Connecting to the Core Sound in Recitative

It's easy to come off the core support of the sound when singing recitative. Young opera singers often make the mistake of lifting off their lower breath support and singing from a high position. While they may completely support their sound while singing arias and duets, their recitatives may be weak and unimpressive because:

1. The text is often faster and not as rhythmically structured as the arias and ensemble pieces. Since it is conversational and more playful, the singer may not give it the gravitas they do with the other music. The recitative is where the story line unfolds and should be treated with just as much importance

as the aria. Don't wait until the last minute to learn recitative. These sections can be the most difficult music to sing and deserve your attention.

2. When singing recitative in a foreign language, the singer can find it hard to connect with their core sound unless guided by a knowledgeable coach on the inflections and stress points of the language. Besides working with a coach, the singer must translate every word to fully understand and express the story line. Once the text makes perfect sense, work the recitative like a monologue (discussed later in this chapter).

3. Acting and stage work can let technique slip. The singer is often concentrating so much on their blocking and memorization that they momentarily forget correct vocal technique.

    To fix, take adequate time to memorize your part. In the real world, the singing artist may be fired if they're not ready to go on day one. During early rehearsals, mark all blocking into the score. Come to rehearsal early before the scene(s) you are working that day and walk the blocking (onstage if possible) as many times as it takes to memorize it so that it doesn't affect your text memory or vocal technique.

4. Being unsure about the modality causes confusion. Chords go by fast in recitative, so if the singer doesn't catch one of the chords, they may come off their sound because they're not sure where the line is taking them. To fix, work with a coach to gain confidence in the harmonic structure and other elements of the recitative. Listen to recordings to memorize the chord changes. Work slowly at first and then pick up the speed.

Recurring Vowels within the Text

Choose a phrase from a song. Circle or highlight each similar vowel in the line, then say the sentence slowly, emphasizing the sound exactly the same for each circled vowel. This process reinforces a consistency of sound and vowel placement. Although this technique can help to line up different vowel sounds in different languages, it works especially well with French schwas.

> ***Exercise:*** *To be consistent pronouncing the schwas in this line from an aria in Jules Massenet's* Manon, *the singer should practice stressing the schwa when reading the line slowly. "É-pou-se quel-que bra-va fil-le, Di-gne de nous, di-gne de twoi." After always coming back to the same schwa sound, increase the speed and then apply to the correct rhythm. Finally, sing the line and notice how this exercise helps maintain a consistent schwa.*

"If your song does not 'take possession of you' before you start, you are subjectively not ready to sing it." —LAMPERTI

UNDERSTANDING AND RESEARCHING THE TEXT

More often than not, students learn the words and notation to the song first, often without putting in the necessary effort of learning word-for-word translations and researching the background of the song. This is a big mistake (one I have made all too often) but is completely understandable due to our many time constraints. However, the effort should be made. Learning the meaning of the text helps the student to visualize the story in their mind's eye, and the researching and understanding of the story behind the lyrics allows the "intent" of the text to naturally dictate correct vocal technique. This helps the student to naturally stress the nouns and action verbs, which helps to anchor the vocal line and produce a more solid core to their tone. And by using double consonants for emphasis, and enunciating vowels and consonants with a more forward placement, the student is able to produce purer vowels, crisper consonants, which allows for better control airflow, dynamics, and shadow vowels.

Relating to the Text

As a student of voice, you have probably already found how important it is to connect emotionally with the text of the song. Although most student singers find this to be one of the last things they get around to when learning a song or aria, it is probably the most important if they are to become musical and move an audience. Most students sing the notes just fine, and can even be proficient in technique, but if they don't believe what they're singing they are only "phoning it in," and neither the singer nor the audience will be completely satisfied. (See "Conscious vs. Unconscious Competence" in Chapter One.)

Intent and Empathy

Expressing the emotions of the text to the audience in as clear and heartfelt a way as possible is the main purpose of singing. Just singing the words is not enough.

The singer's emotional connection with the text almost always dictates how well they can sing the song. Believing the message of the text allows the singer to naturally attack a phrase or stress certain words with the intent of the text, giving them better breath control, vowel placement, and diction. It also allows the performer to engage and connect with the audience, making the performance more believable.

This intent, however, is hard to find without a bit of empathy with the text's meaning and the reason the composer/poet composed it. Relating to the emotion behind the song's text is essential in bringing life to the music and bringing your audience into the moment, and this is not often possible without some kind of research.

Researching the Text

1. Word-for-Word Translation: If the song is in a foreign language, you must first interpret exactly what the text means. As mentioned earlier, most foreign language songs do place an English "transliteration" of the text directly beneath the Italian or whatever language the piece is in. But this is only a representation of the foreign language in your own language; it's not the exact translation of each individual word. And it's written so the singer can perform the song in their own language using the correct syntax and sentence structure.

   But if the performer wants to give a true interpretation of the text, it's helpful to know the real meaning of each word so the singer can then stress the nouns and action verbs to anchor the vocal line and bring a more solid core to the tone. This is also accomplished with the use of double consonants such as "I llove you" instead of "I love you." Which one would you believe more? But better yet, know and believe what you are saying, and the stresses will be there naturally. Empathy with the emotion and meaning of the song is only possible if you know exactly what you're saying.

2. Time Period/Life Event/Location: What was the lyricist/poet thinking when the song was written? Had they just lost their spouse to some disease, or had the death of one of their children prompted the writing of those sad words? It makes a big difference in your interpretation. What year is it? Where are you located? Who are you singing to? Also, if the song is part of a bigger composition such as a song cycle, a musical, or an opera, how does your song relate in context with the whole piece?

The emotional intent of the text should be seen in the face and in the actions of the performer, so it helps to have a sensitive and imaginative insight into the text. You should truly comprehend what the poet is saying and know the piece so well that spontaneity, not choreographed facial expressions and gestures, will spring forth naturally. On this matter of spontaneity, Shirlee Emmons summarized "a favorite thought" of the famous Russian theater director Konstantin Stanislavski:

> *A singer is more fortunate than an actor. The composer provides him with the rhythm of his inner emotions. Actors must create this for themselves out of a vacuum. The singing actor listens to the inner rhythm of his song and makes it his own. The written word is the author's theme, but the music is the emotional experience of that theme. (p. 114)*

As soon as you have gotten to know what your text is all about, I personally suggest learning the text as a monologue (in any language), and then acting it out. As the late Shirlee Emmons said, "Why must one be an actor when performing songs? Because there are words."

Working It Like a Monologue

This is a wonderful device for getting to know the true meaning of the text. Though it takes longer when working in a foreign language, this exercise nonetheless helps the student feel what's happening in the song. Speak and move about and act it out as you would if you were in a play. Blocking your movements also help. Being at specific locations onstage, turning your head, or looking at something simultaneously with the music also helps to ingrain the words in your memory. If you're able to perform your song as if in a play, you're ready to perform the song in recital. You may not be able to move around in performance as much as in rehearsal, but you'll see these movements in your mind's eye, and this will solidify the text.

> "The physiological singing tone evolves from the speaking voice.... Phonetic vibrations felt at lips, nose, head, throat and chest carry distinct messages to every part of the body. These messages are recorded in the singer's consciousness until habitual reaction takes the place of effort and thought." —LAMPERTI

MEMORIZATION

The job of memorizing a piece of music is handled a bit differently by every singer. One may have photographic memory—in Beverly: An Autobiography, Beverly Sills (1987) said she could "learn an opera in hours"—but most of us aren't lucky enough to have that ability. All of our brains are wired a little differently and some of us just remember things better and more quickly than others. I find, though, that the more time I spend on memorizing dialogue or lyrics, the better I get at it. Some people make a game out of it, which helps them memorize faster. For me, visual, rhythmic, and blocking cues work best. I would like to share a few suggestions that have worked for me.

Visually

When I'm on the go, I'm usually running lyrics through my head as I walk or drive. I often find that I can't remember a key word or two in the line. The last thing I want to do is stick in some random word just to go on with the rest of the song (too many times repeating a wrong word in the text hardwires it in the memory). Instead of stopping and pulling out my score, finding the right page with the word, then putting away the music and continuing on my way, I have taken the time to write out all the lyrics on index cards and have them conveniently in my front pocket, where I can reference them on the go.

Buy some index cards (small enough to fit a pocket) and at least two different colored pens for this. You could use your smartphone with word processing, but the cards seem to work best and are not as distracting in the car (holding your phone while driving may be illegal in your state, anyway). After choosing the song you are memorizing:

1. Start writing the first phrase on the blank side of the card with black ink. If it's the first verse, mark it with the number 1. (You get much more text on a card that is turned sideways so that it is taller than it is wide.)
2. Below that first phrase, if the text is in a language you don't know, use the colored pen to write the word-for-word translation. Continue this process down the card. Another option, if you know the language already, is to mark the rhythm of the text below in a different color.
3. Notice and mark (with an asterisk or different color) when certain phrases are repeated (who wants to waste time on a phrase again if you've already learned it earlier in the song?).
4. Indent sections that are different in the song such as the chorus or when the B or C section comes in. You could also use a different color for each section to make them stand out.

Remember, it's all about what the card looks like visually. That way, when you're onstage trying to remember the text, the look of the card and the different colors pop into your head.

Rhythmically

Knowing the exact rhythm of the song not only helps to engrain the text into the brain, it helps to keep the breath support solid. Slopping through triplets and dotted note patterns and being behind or jumping a beat makes the voice insecure and keeps the singer from completely engaging in good vocal technique. Here are a few ways to practice rhythm.

1. Tap or clap the rhythm.
2. Speak the rhythm. Example: One, two, three-and-a, four. One-and-a, two-and-a, three, four, etc.
3. La-la the rhythm. Until you have the rhythm down, don't even try incorporating the words.
4. Write the rhythm on an index card above the words (as in #2 of the last exercise).

Blocking

Blocking is very helpful in the memorization process, especially when learning an operatic or musical theater role. Although the singer should be totally off book by the time rehearsals get to the blocking stage, once blocking is started, the position onstage is an extra reminder of where you are in the score. This is one of the reasons singers usually use their score in a concert performance, because there are no blocking references to remind the singer where they are in the music.

FIVE

The Body Connection

"If preparing to sing does not straighten you up like a soldier, some essential part of your anatomy is not taking part." —Lamperti

One of the most overlooked aspects to a good singing technique is posture and how it affects the voice. Leaning on one leg, jutting the head forward, slumping the shoulders, and an array of other incorrect positioning wreak havoc on sound production. Poor posture not only puts the vocal tract out of alignment, it incorrectly distributes or diminishes energy to the muscles needed for good breath support.

POSTURE/ALIGNMENT

Basically, a good body alignment, or what *bel canto* calls "The Noble Position," means that:

- The shoulders are back and relaxed.
- The sternum is high.
- The neck straight (jaw neither tilting up or compressing down).

- An even balance of the torso on both legs with the knees unlocked.
- Feet are a shoulder's width apart.

However, there are a number of alignment methods used by musicians and actors that may help free and develop fluidly aligned body movement.

Alexander Technique: The technique of changing faulty posture habits, improving mobility and alertness, and relieving chronic stiffness, tension, and stress. Developed by Frederick Matthias Alexander (1869–1955).

The Feldenkreis Method: Described as "an internal journey to rediscover balance, flexibility and coordination." Founded by Dr. Mosche Feldenkreis, there are two facets to this method: awareness through movement and functional integration.

The Trager Approach: The method of triggering tissue changes by using sensory-motor feedback loops such as pleasurable or positive feelings between the mind and muscles. Founded by Milton Trager, M.D.

T'ai Chi Ch'uan: Both a type of self-defense and slow-motion exercise that circulates vital forces (chi) through the body for longevity and health. Developed by Chang San Feng about seven hundred years ago, this exercise balances body energy (chi).

Rolfing: Realignment of the body by manipulating and readjusting the muscle fascia. Everyone has one or more traumatic events in their life that make the body tense up. This causes a chemical reaction that makes the fascia sticky, causing the muscles to freeze in position and pulling the body out of alignment. A rolfer kneads and elbows between this stuck fascia, causing them to release and relax back to their normal state, bringing the body back into alignment. Developed by biochemist Ida Rolf between 1917 and 1927.

"Your song is born of your imagination. Your technique springs from your thoughts. Your interpretation is molded by your emotion which welds imagination and thought together."—LAMPERTI

EMOTIONAL ALIGNMENT

If the head is facing one direction and the torso another, there is tension and compression of the neck. This often happens in performance when the singer allows an emotional urge to quickly move the head in a certain direction without following it with the body. This will cause a problem with even sound production. Of course, it's important to feel the text with emotion, but it should never be at the detriment of vocal alignment.

To fix, practice turning your head quickly from left to right, allowing the body to follow in that direction immediately after. Do not turn the body at the exact time the head turns, as this is a sign of tension and looks like your neck is fused, giving you the "Frankenstein" look. However, if and when the head jerks in a direction, the body must immediately follow, keeping the vocal track in alignment.

Singing into the Floor

Something interesting happens to many singers when they get emotionally involved singing about something or someone during a performance or audition. There's often a tendency to start singing at the floor in a self-reflective or contemplative fashion. I know, because I used to do it all the time. What I believed was perceived as emotionally strong to the audience really wasn't. All it did was project the sound into the floor or orchestra pit instead of out into the theater. This action also scrunches the chin down and affects the singer's vocal tract, closing down their sound.

This was a wonderful fix I learned in a masterclass with the great baritone Thomas Hampson. Spread your arms wide and start walking backward as you sing your aria or art song. Immediately the head is up, the sternum is up, the voice opens up, and the alignment is fixed.

STANCE

A strong stance and solid connection to the floor help the singer connect to their core sound and low breath support. Carrying a high sternum and straight neck helps keep the flow of air to the vocal mechanism open and free. Here is a fix to help the singer find that strong connection to their core sound.

This fix was also taken from a masterclass with Thomas Hampson, and I use it all the time. First, sing a phrase you want to improve. Then, while standing solidly on both feet, pull back one foot at a time, and then stick the ball of the foot into the floor (you've seen baseball players do this at bat). This connects you to the floor and to your solid base. Now, stand tall and try the phrase again. You're likely to find that the voice will be stronger and more connected to the core sound.

EXTERNAL CAUSES OF POOR POSTURE

Often alignment can be negatively impacted by conditions such as heavy costuming, high heels, or a raked stage. The singer must be conscious of any vocal problems developing during rehearsal that may cause these conditions, and then work it out with their dresser, director, and/or voice teacher before the first performance.

> *"If the top falls out of your tone, you have uprooted your energy from the pelvic region."* —LAMPERTI

PELVIC TILT

Most singers have good alignment and a healthy muscle tension relationship between their torso and pelvis. But those who don't, those with an exaggerated curve to the lower back, need to compensate for this misalignment by tilting or "tucking" the pelvis forward. I've found that this applies more to female students than male students. By tilting the pelvis forward, the singer will improve their range of motion to their diaphragm and engage underactive abdominal muscles, hopefully improving their breath support system. Tucking also seems to be helpful in unlocking the knees when the pelvis is in the most favorable position.

This pelvic tilt my come naturally for singers who have trained as dancers to subconsciously grip their buttocks and keep their pelvis forward. That's great, but remember, the pelvis area should be able to move freely, allowing for better support and breath management.

MUSCLE MEMORY AND HABIT FORMATION

Muscle memory is the result of repetition. It's why we practice so hard to improve our voices. Repetition of correct vocal technique while practicing vocalises, breathing exercises, word preparation, vocal gymnastics, and many other aspects of singing helps coordinate a unified and balanced vocal mechanism.

Developing a professional singing voice takes years of practice and repetition. And the hours of (correct) practice correlates exactly with how fast the singer improves. You may have heard the formula that 10,000 hours of practice (or a little over three hours a day for ten years) allows one to master what they're working on. In music that would include time spent on all things related to your voice, such as sight reading, learning music theory, vocal pedagogy, and ensemble rehearsal, to name a few.

THE HEAD

Relaxing and freeing the face from entanglements and tension should involve "mirror" work. Get in front of a mirror and monitor all the things that can go wrong. Here are a few:

> **Forehead Tension:** Raising the eyebrows and wrinkling the forehead when reaching for high notes are not going to help the student improve their singing. Of course, this facial tension is usually a result of high breathing and upper body tension. Here's how to keep an expressive face without the tension:
>
> Practice in front of the mirror by working the song like a monologue. How would your face express the text if you were speaking it instead of singing it? See what your facial expressions looks like in the mirror by first speaking the text with a supported stage voice. Now try singing phrases of the song with the same expression and support. With expression there will be a more forward lip placement. This is good unless it looks strange. It's good for airflow and resonance, but if used too much it will create tension and a strained look, so adjust accordingly until you are expressive yet relaxed. There is nothing worse than to have a deadpan face when you're in front of an audience.
>
> **Lip Tension:** For years I had a trembly upper lip, which I would pull down over my top teeth, especially when reaching

for higher notes. The top lip shaking or both lips puckering too much is caused by tension in the lips and should be worked out before you sing (see "Gross Chewing" at the end of this chapter), along with working out jaw and tongue tension. You can also grab your lips with your fingers and rub the tension out. Remember, there does have to be engagement in the lips for acoustical reasons, and it does take time to build the singing embrasure, but the lips should be free to relax and smile when needed.

Effects of Smiling: Learn to smile with your eyes. As I have mentioned throughout this book, the acoustical need for engaging the lips restricts the time allowed for open mouth smiling, which should only happen during rests and breaks in the music. The negative effect that spreading the mouth has on tone quality is major and has to be avoided at all costs.

Natural Effects on the Voice

All people have the same basic equipment inside their vocal tract, and unless there is some severe vocal or hearing impediment, most people can be trained to sing. It's basically like going to the gym, where the muscles are built and taught to coordinate with each other. With the right voice teacher and enough practice, not everyone will become a master singer, but all will show marked improvement. Here are some factors that aren't normally talked about that can also have an effect on the voice:

Genetics: Individuals have slight variations in the size of vocal folds, larynx, skulls, and cheek bones. The physical attributes you inherit from your parents can all be factors in how naturally resonant and beautiful a voice can sound. Through training and compensation some of this can be nullified (or enhanced), but because we want as natural a sound as possible when singing, these physical discrepancies will make a difference in sound to some effect.

Five singers may be learning the same techniques from the same voice teacher, but just like five different handmade violins may have similar shapes, there will be a slight difference between all five instruments. These are reflected in some of singers having a more acoustically perfect space within the mouth and throat than others. Not everyone is a natural Stradivarius, but with correct technique, formant tuning, practice, and a good ear many students can achieve great achievements with their voice.

Environment: Another factor that may have an effect on the voice is the environment the singer is raised in. A perfect example would be a baby that is raised around smoking parents. I've known a number of students who find it almost impossible to breathe in quickly and deeply because their parents were chain smokers. Can you imagine getting your diapers changed as your mother's cigarette ash dangles above you ready to fall? Needless to say, these students grew up avoiding deep inhalation of smoke and have gotten used to only using half of their lung power.

Mental: As I covered extensively in Chapter One, the psychology of singing is paramount when it comes to singing well. How the singer thinks can be a huge destabilizer. For example, stage fright may be caused from some bad early experiences and a sense of inferiority brought on by unthinking parents or friends. However, a positive attitude and encouragement from the voice teacher can be huge when building confidence and the right attitude toward an enjoyable singing experience. Personally, I find the mental process of singing to be one of the most interesting aspects in teaching voice.

"Do not listen to yourself sing. Feel yourself sing!" —LAMPERTI

The Ears

Hearing vs. Listening vs. Feeling

Hearing. The physical reaction we have to sound is a result of how we perceive it. The natural response to "hearing" a sound is often involuntary and does not engage in the thinking process more than acknowledging it with a knee-jerk physical reaction or programmed vocal response. Since we were born, our perception of life events, brought on by the different senses, has brought these reactionary responses. Many are instinctual, but often these responses have been initiated and eventually developed through repetition. This reactionary muscle memory is what we've felt is needed to survive, or at least navigate, certain life events. In singing, however, "hearing" is not enough. There must be a higher, developed level of sensitivity involved with the aural process.

Listening: When it comes to "listening" we have intellectually and empathetically developed the ability to not only hear the sound, but also to analyze the meaning, feel the physical sensations, and determine a course of action. We've done this by either growing up around good singing and music, or trusting in our voice teacher's ears, then emulating their perception of a genuinely good vocal tone until all our vocal functions are balanced and consistent. We learn, imitate, and repeat until our ears, the feeling associated to resonant sound, and the singing technique are well tempered. Then, once mastered, we go back to trusting our "hearing's" reactionary impulses and our technique and no longer feel the need to intellectualize and justify every sound we make. We can have fun with it!

But "listening" isn't that easy. To trust in someone else's opinion and realize that the sound one is used to making may be flawed can be a shock to one's self-image. The student may think that the teacher is trying to change their personality. In that case the student has to understand why having a realistic and positive self-concept of their own voice is so important. The student must know that being with an objective, impartial listener with much experience is the only way to receive immediate feedback and truly monitor and tweak the voice in real time. It's the main purpose behind having a voice teacher.

Feeling: The student should understand that the sound they hear and what the teacher hears are different. Hearing one's own voice through the head's internal bone conduction creates a distorted aural impression that is different than what others hear. Actually, since sound passes through bone half as quickly as air, lower frequencies are enhanced and higher frequencies are reduced, causing the voice to sound bigger to the person who is singing. The student must therefore "trust" the feeling created through disciplined experimentation and good technique with assistance from their teacher. The student should try to remember the tactile "feeling" of the correct connection to the cords, the placement of the sound, and the ring (*squillo*) in the voice. This is also the only way there will be a consistency of sound made in any size of venue. There's a great tendency for the singer to push when on the large stage or outdoors in order to match the sound created in the practice room or smaller theater. But when the technique is secure, "feeling" the sound will keep the singer's voice balanced and acoustically focused.

Hear It Before You Sing It

The ability to hear the note sequence or tune in the head before singing, coined *audiation* by Edwin Gordon (1927–2015) in 1975, is essential to pitch, resonance, and all aspects of good singing. Gordon suggests that "audiation is to music what thought is to language." In fact, along with individual experience and knowledge, this type of aural perception is a major factor in musical learning, successful practice, and development of musical aptitude (Gordon More, 2020).

Does the singer know the song well enough to sing it through without accompaniment? Do they wake up with the tune playing in their head or catch themselves humming it out of the blue? If not, they don't know the melody well enough. So, when attempting to perform the song, this will cause hesitation even if they are looking at the music. And if they're working hard at sight reading or remembering the melody, they're going to forget technical aspects such as correct breathing, double consonants, or resonance placement (formant tuning). The better the singer knows the song, the better they will sing it.

But what if the ear just doesn't hear it? And what happens when the singer thinks they know it but has problems finding the correct pitch correlation between notes?

> *"The ear is true only through team-work of thought and imagination."* —LAMPERTI

Pitch

While a singer may have the most beautiful tone, great resonance, good diction, and best intensions, if they have poor pitch, they will not have a career in singing.

Professional singing does not just mean having good "pipes," but also means having a good ear. This means coordination between the voice, ear, and brain. That is to say, the sound waves made by the vibrator (vocal folds) creates nerve impulses that are converted by hair cells in the cochlea of the ear, which are then stored and evaluated by the brain in its temporal lobe's auditory cortex. If there is miscommunication or poor coordination during any of this process, there is a possibility the singer may have pitch problems. Also, according to Reid (1983), since the auditory cortex plays an important role in musical imagery (hearing a sound in one's head) and the short-term memory of musical sounds, poor pitch often is a result of misuse or underuse of that part of the brain during the development of the body (though one can't rule out genetic causes).

There are four different levels of pitch ability:

Perfect Pitch: The mind of a musician with perfect or absolute pitch has the long-term memory to remember the acoustic feeling and auditory vibration of any given pitch and the ability to repeat it at any time. This can be a blessing and a curse for those singers who have it. Many of the musicians and instruments they work with may be slightly out of tune or tuned too low or high. The singer will then have to either adjust to their tuning or sound out of tune themselves relative to the other musicians. Perfect pitch is fairly rare (less than 1 in 10,000) and is learned at a very early age. But, according to Jann Ingmire (May 28, 2015), it's possible to teach some adults, with training lasting for months. "[A] 2013 study from Harvard University researchers reported that a drug commonly used to treat epilepsy could effectively reopen a critical period of learning ability, allowing a person to learn skills like absolute pitch." And that even without drugs, "[a] UChicago study trained participants to identify piano notes by sound alone, demonstrating that absolute pitch can be a learned skill."

Relative Pitch: The mind knows the given pitch is relatively near to where it thinks it is. Professional singers with this type of pitch are the most common and have the ability to immediately hear when they're in tune, relative to the tuning of the instrument(s) they are singing with, or relative to the intervals of the key or mode they are in.

Poor Pitch: Caused by poor technique or poorly developed vocal apparatus. This may also be a result of underdeveloped listening skills. This problem can be fixed and will be discussed in Chapter Six.

Forget about it! The total inability to sing on pitch could be a miscommunication between voice, ear, and brain or may be the result of Asperger's syndrome (see Appendix I). The singer is totally tone-deaf and has no concept of pitch, where the note is relative to other notes, or whether they are singing high or low. Though some of this can be taught over time with a lot of repetition, the ability to be able to sing a song a capella is almost impossible. Students who show no ability in matching pitches should be encouraged to pursue a different vocation. But that doesn't mean they shouldn't keep singing in their own shower. They can still have fun trying.

Imitation

As I explained in Chapter One, you only sing as beautiful a tone as you can imagine. This is relevant when speaking of imitation, or the ability to mimic a sound or voice of an animal or another human. Professional impersonators have trained themselves to recognize inflections in the voice of, say, a famous personality, along with the tone, depth, and diction of their voices. This ability of impersonation comes easier for some than others, but most can be trained once they know what to look for.

The ability to imitate singing voices, and specifically the qualities that make a fine voice, is also possible. Studying great singer's breathing techniques, their onset to a phrase, and their vowel placement, among other aspects, is a great education for any singer, and one that is too often overlooked by the young singer.

Operatic baritone Titta Ruffo (1877–1953), one of the most famous singers of the early twentieth century, grew up in Italy listening to and imitating great singers, many of whom were his relatives and neighbors. Living in this musical environment, where singing was just a part of life, educated his ear and helped him develop naturally as a great singer. Because the popular opera repertoire of the day was his favorite music to listen to, he instinctively adjusted his voice to reflect his favorite singer's resonant tone, musical inflections, and diction to a point where he surpassed them in beauty and strength. And although his career was not as long lived as it could have been (he was self-taught and hadn't learned healthy vocal technique), his ability to imitate the positive qualities of a well-trained voice was undeniable.

The ability to imitate all types of sounds is useful. As a child I was raised on a five-acre farm outside of Sioux Falls, South Dakota, and we had many different kinds of animals. I learned to imitate roosters crowing, cows mooing, pigs oinking, sheep baaing, dogs barking, and owls hooting. I didn't know it at the time, but I was learning to use all the spaces in the nooks and crannies of my vocal tract, lowering the larynx when needed and accessing spaces in my sinuses to achieve the necessary inflections to make my voice sound like my barnyard friends. I later realized that imitating them was helpful in my vocal training, so I now help young singers find at least a few things they can imitate well.

Imitation is also useful in the study of extreme speech variations made by cartoon characters on TV or the exaggerated speech of people who are drunk or insane. The range of inflection in these voices is absolutely amazing, and quite relevant to using the singing voice. Intensive listening and imitation of these kind of vocal inflections can teach the beginning singer to find the spaces in their vocal tract so they may later express emotion in the songs they sing. Voice-over (VO) professionals, those voice actors who make a living with their spoken voice on radio/TV ad commercials, recorded books, and video games, also use a large range of vocal inflection. Professional singers often find that using their voice doing voice-overs is a rewarding experience.

THE HANDS

Hand Movements During Practice

As was explained in Chapter Three, at first it is hard to internalize vocal technique without some external help. Instrumentalists depress keys, strings, and valves to sound a note, but singers don't have the advantage of touch when trying to produce a sound. They are, however, able to use hand gestures and body movements to help learn certain aspects of singing such as vocal onset, keeping time, phrasing, and the connection of sound. Breath coordination and attack of the note can be developed much faster when using the hand and arm as a visual and tactile aid. Using arm and hand movements gives the singer a sense of coordination with the breath, engrains the feeling of exact placement and forward movement, and encourages the whole body to be part of the singing process. After using this technique in practice to help recognize the correct feeling in the body, we can then internalize the process and stop using the hand movements while performing.

In order for the voice to release freely, the air has to move with no hesitation or obstruction, which means having a relaxed throat while engaging and energizing attitude/intent behind the breath. The singer has to get used to "throwing the voice away" or "letting the voice fly," and in so doing balance the breath by getting rid of excess subglottal air. The use of hands to aid this process can be very helpful.

Toward the end of Chapter Three I presented exercises on how to balance the breath. They were "Throwing the Ball," "Tennis," "Frisbee," "Fishing," and "Skipping the Rock." Here are two other ways to balance the breath while using the hands. Allow the breath to be taken in on the uptake of the arm, and then released with a "fling" of the arm and hand, allowing the breath to leave the body freely:

Shoot the Pistol: Pretending to shoot the first note by pulling back the arm (while taking a low inhalation) and then throwing the index finger forward (on an "h" or soft consonant) with the snap (and tone) being placed exactly on the beat. For exactness of the snap, try touching your finger on a hard surface when engaging the tone. The tactile reference of the touch will make sure that you're starting the tone right where you want it, not too late and not too early.

Throw the Dart: Pretending to throw a dart with the thumb and index finger also works. Pull back the arm (with a low breath), throw the pretend dart with arm forward (on an "h" or soft consonant), then open the fingers and release the dart exactly on the beat (and tone).

The following exercises help connect and support the vocal line through legato and the use of *appoggio*.

Icing the Cake: While singing an "ah" on a glide, scale, or arpeggio, pretend to spread icing on a cake with your fingers.

Ice Skating: On a slow upward glide, imagine you're out on the ice skating down a river or long track. Or, imagine pushing off and feeling the glide on the ice between notes, as you ascend on a glide up and down. Rock the body and swing the arms, as if during ice skating or Rollerblading, just to get your body feeling it.

The Motorcycle Throttle: If you know how to ride a motorcycle, pretend to pull back on the throttle with your right hand and then relax, like you're gunning the engine. Now attach an "ah" and vocalize up (as you pull back on the throttle) and down (as you release the throttle). Just play with small and large intervals and vary the speed as you do it. Keep the throat open, and as you go up to higher and higher notes, think lower and lower into your breath support. For fast leaps there should be a quick kick out with the lower abdominal muscles.

Pointing Down While Going Up: As you ascend on a glide up to a high note using an "ah," the higher you go, the more the necessity to compensate for the throat wanting to clamp up. Instead of thinking up to the note, drop the jaw and think down as you point your finger forward and down. It's just like an inflection, so consider the top and bottom notes as the top and bottom of a circle and just connect the sound instead of thinking up and down.

Walking the Table: As explained in Chapter Three, this exercise has the singer push their finger forward along the edge of a table or piano after taking a nice low breath to sing or vocalize. By concentrating on the forward movement of the finger, the breath should stay very connected and be able to support the voice till the end of the phrase. The intent behind this forward movement may not always be controlled by the meaning of the text, but should always be controlled by an underlying attitude and intensity in order to keep the air moving forward fast enough to maintain pitch and intensity. This is vital in helping the singer be their most expressive.

Hand Movements While Performing

Of course, using our hands in performance as we do in practice would look strange at the very least. Hands, however, are a major component in communicating with the audience, so the singer has to learn to use them expressively. To accomplish this, I highly recommend that all singers take acting and movement classes. One of the most respected is the Wesley Balk Opera/Musical Theater Institute (http://www.wesleybalk.org). Workshops like this help build upon the basic skills of singing by incorporating acting and movement and unifying the essential musical and theatrical components into an integrated performance.

In the meantime, here are a few things to think about when using your hands during a performance.

1. Never let arms and hands just hang at your sides.
2. Keep elbows close to the body except when reaching.

3. Try not to spread the fingers.
4. Never lock elbows. Keep one or both arms moving at all times.

Learning to use the arms and hands will truly free the singer to express themselves onstage. But much of this expression comes instinctively once a good technique is established and the nerves don't get in the way. Just as hand movements become natural when we speak, the hands as we sing should be an extension of the performer's personality expressing itself via the song's text.

BODY WARM UPS

Just as in sports, building coordinated, strong muscles in the singing apparatus is achieved by conscious repetitive movement. The vocal cords and muscles for breath support and lung capacity must be built up over days, months, and years by consistent and dedicated practice. This develops the muscle memory needed for good vocal technique. But first, the total body has to be relaxed and free to move.

As I said earlier in this book, many vocal problems in the vocal tract are a result of imbalance or tension taking place in another part of the body. The following are a set of warm-ups I use with all my students to free up that tension in the body so that imbalance doesn't take place. They only take five minutes or so, but should not be skipped over in a rush to get practicing. I find that it's best to do the following exercises in succession. Both singers and their teachers should always be conscious of physical limitations and adjust these exercises accordingly.

Head Rolls: Stand straight with feet about two feet apart, shoulders back, and chin level. Drop the chin and slowly roll the head to the left as you start to count to four. One is at nine o'clock, two at six o'clock, three at three o'clock, and four straight ahead. Repeat three more times. Then do the same to the right, rolling the head with one at three o'clock and so on for four repetitions.

Shoulder Figure Eights: Taking the left shoulder first, slowly draw the shape of the number 8, four times. Repeat with the right shoulder. Take your time and try to catch all the turns of the 8 with the shoulder. It takes a little while to get coordinated with this, but it feels great when those muscles are stretching and cracking.

Bend to the Floor: Position your body as you did with the head rolls. Starting with the chin dropping, slowly drop vertebrae by vertebrae until your hands touch the floor (palms if you can). Just relax and let your head and hands hang while you keep breathing low into your diaphragm. Feel the back muscles and everything stretch. Stay there at least ten seconds, just letting go. Remember, keep breathing! Now, slowly and from the hips, come back up vertebrae by vertebrae until your chin is even to the floor.

Repeat this exercise. Make sure it is done exactly the same, only this time with a faster drop. When you're hanging there, bounce a little or walk your hands out in front to stretch even further. Keep breathing, then after ten seconds return to the starting position.

Relaxing the Jaw and Tongue: I can't emphasize enough the importance of stretching out the jaw before singing. Your practice will improve immensely. More about jaw and tongue tension and their detriment to good singing can be found in Chapter Two.

Rubbing Out the Jaw: Right in front of the ear is the temporomandibular joint, or TMJ. A great deal of tension builds up there from chewing and talking, so it's good to help relax that joint before singing. Using the index and middle fingers on both hands, drop your jaw and feel where that TMJ is. Now gently rub out the joint with your fingers for a couple of minutes to release tension and stress.

Gross Chewing: Here's a great exercise to loosen up and get rid of jaw and tongue tension. I never start singing without doing this one.

1. Open the mouth as tall and wide as possible.
2. Pull back on the lips and hold (all the muscles in the neck will get tight).
3. Then close the mouth and pucker the lips.
4. Go back and forth from those two positions saying "Mwah, Mwah."
5. After three or four times hold the mouth in the open position and stick out the tongue as far as possible.
6. Rock the tongue from left to right a few times.

In the following chapter we will be dealing with the singing student's need for a qualified voice teacher, what to look for in a teacher, how to practice, the dos and don'ts for singers, as well as fixes for common vocal problems.

SIX

The Teacher Connection

For the serious student of voice to be fairly proficient, vocal study takes from three to six years (it's actually a lifetime endeavor for the professional singer), starting in earnest in their freshman to sophomore year of high school. But there is so much more to vocal music than singing. Having taken piano since the age of six, and playing saxophone since nine, I know how important it is to be a well-rounded musician. When I was in college there was this well-known joke by instrumentalists who would ask singers "What are you? A musician or a singer?" They got a big kick out of that. But you know what? They were right. Way too many "singers" are missing vital pieces of a musical education.

That's why I have always insisted that a prospective voice student have at least one year of piano study before they start private voice lessons and encourage them to sing in a choir if they can. It's important to be a well-rounded musician to get into this business. The ability to sight-read and play piano and/or another instrument is crucial for the student planning to make singing their career.

FINDING THE RIGHT VOICE TEACHER

If a person has the call (yes, it is a calling) to pursue singing as their profession, they will need all the help they can get, and that means getting the best teacher possible. To be a professional singer or improve the voice to a level adequate enough to sing competently, the student needs a teacher they can trust, who puts the student's best interests first, and who is able to help that student find their full vocal potential. How do you avoid throwing away thousands of dollars on con men/women who may talk convincingly but lack the needed teaching experience or background?

AATS Voice Teacher Guidelines. According to the American Academy of Teachers of Singing (AATS), voice teachers require specific qualifications in order to teach beginner through professional singing at the highest level. I'm including these qualifications in full to help the new voice student avoid poor choices.

The following two lists of qualifications will help serious students of classical music and musical theater choose a proficient voice teacher. Written by the National Music Council of the AATS and originally published in 1975 (updated in its present form in 1997) as "Qualifications for Teachers of Singing," this guideline lays out the skills teachers should have in teaching classical and musical theater students:

1. A thorough general and musical education, including sight-singing and ear training. A teacher must be musically literate.
2. A substantial background in vocal study with competent teachers of singing over a period of at least five years. Musical and vocal instruction should include a minimum of 90 hours each year.
3. A complete anatomical knowledge of the body (not just the vocal tract), because the vocal system relies on the whole-body support system for the production of tone. For too many

decades many have relied on phrases passed from studio to studio, generation to generation. Students repeat these phrases like mottos, not truly understanding the semantic implications nor the physical follow-through. Books or models of the entire anatomy should be used in teaching, to make clear the actual positions and possible functions of the organs and muscles.

4. An overview of the contiguous arts and therapies that can ease tensions and aid in such things as posture control, i.e., Alexander Technique, Feldenkrais Method, Rosen Method, massage therapies, dancing fencing, acting, etc.

5. Sensitivity to accuracy of intonation, quality of tone, and nuance of color.

6. A broad knowledge of vocal repertory, and styles of interpretation appropriate to opera, oratorio, art song, ballad, folk, song, and musical theater. (Note: Have the prospective teacher sing you a part of the same song in three different styles and have them explain what makes each style sound different.)

7. Ability to classify a voice. It is generally acknowledged that this important decision dare not be taken hastily. Younger voices take their own time to develop since the larynx itself is still in the formative stage. Correct teaching will allow the voice to reveal its own classification. Caveat: one should not assign music too demanding for the sensitive voice, i.e., freshman voices should not sing senior music.

8. A thorough knowledge and command of the English language; complete mastery of English diction in song through correct articulation, enunciation, and pronunciation; a knowledge of at least three languages (Italian, German, and French) encompassing basic grammar and good performance diction.

9. A basic understanding of psychology and its effective use in the teaching of singing, including a sympathetic, discerning, and analytical approach to both personal and professional problems of the student.
10. The ability to demonstrate with his or her own voice the correct principles of good tone production and interpretation. (It must be remembered that many successful and prominent teachers have not been established vocal performers, and many noted singers have not achieved success as teachers.)
11. Some competence at the piano.

The whole future of a singer may be ruined by incorrect teaching in the beginning; therefore choose your teacher with as much care as you would your doctor. The following list, also written by the AATS (1997), informs the new student on what to avoid when looking for a voice teacher.

- Avoid – teachers who make extravagant promises and beguile by flattery.
- Avoid – teachers who advertise themselves as "the greatest living authority."
- Avoid – teachers who claim the discovery of new and wonderful methods.
- Avoid – teachers who promise results in a short or specified time. Singing is a physical development in which muscles are trained to coordinate. This takes time and varies with each individual.
- Avoid – teachers who claim to teach the method of some well-known artist with whom they have never studied, or with whom they have studied for only a few sessions.

- Avoid – teachers who offer a few tricks as a "cure-all" for vocal ills.
- Remember – that the most effective teaching requires personal contact, close observation, and constant reiteration.
- Remember – that a beautiful natural voice is no more valuable to its possessor than a beautiful violin or piano. It is just as difficult to master one as the other. A singer must be trained, no matter how beautiful the natural voice.
- Remember – that a thorough musical foundation, authoritative languages, and general culture are indispensable.
- Remember – that intelligence, diligence, determination, vigorous health, and adequate financial resources are necessary for the student of singing.
- Remember – that there is no quick result in the study of singing. The student should be prepared for an extended period of study. This does not exclude the possibility of earning money by singing within this period.
- Remember – that a career in singing is one of enormous difficulty, in which few achieve success.

Now that you know what to look for, where do you start looking? Here are a few recommendations:

1. Call local university music departments to get names of grad students and professors who provide private lessons.
2. Inquire at the local music theater, opera company, or fine arts center office or greenroom.
3. Check with local music stores. They usually have a list of teachers.
4. If you're in a choir, ask the director if they know of any teachers.

5. Online sources such as TakeLessons.com show you teachers in your area and show the teacher's qualifications and background. Though I highly recommend taking lessons at the teacher's studio, many teachers also give you the option of taking lessons remotely via online video conferencing platforms such as Zoom, Skype, and others.

After finding a teacher, set up a half-hour or hour-long assessment lesson where you can see how well the two of you work together. This is also the time to ask all the questions you have. The teacher will use this time to decide if they want to work with you, too, so the assessment lesson is sort of an audition. Some of the things they will want to know are:

1. What kind of vocal range do you have? They will work you up to the highest and lowest ends of your voice.
2. They will have you sing a short piece of your choice to get an idea about your tonal quality, musicality, and stage personality.
3. How well you match pitches. The teacher will pluck out a succession of notes on the piano and have you sing back the notes on some nonsense syllable like "la."
4. They will then give you a short lesson to see how well you take instruction and if you have a good sense of concentration.
5. At the end of the lesson they will then give you advice on what vocal problems to work on, your approximate voice type, what kind of repertoire to work on, and some goals to shoot for, i.e., a game plan.

Unless you work it out with the teacher beforehand, expect to pay for this assessment lesson. If you both decide that the two of you work well together, the teacher will probably expect at least a three-month time commitment of either a half-hour or full-hour lesson per week, to be paid according to their policy or whatever you agree upon.

VOCAL RANGE

One of the most-asked questions by young singers is that of range. "If I can sing an E2 up to a E7, what am I?" It seems like they are all obsessed with what range they are, even when they haven't taken any lessons. Seven out of ten of them think they already have amazing ranges, sometimes up to six octaves wide. Most beginners have no idea whether to include vocal fry, falsetto, or the whistle register in the range estimate and rarely include the tone's timbre as part of the determination. Also, many of these curious beginners are in their early teens and have not developed the voice enough to give a true estimation of vocal type. With all the popular vocal talent shows on TV and extreme use of falsetto and belt by pop and rock singers, many young singers are very confused, and I don't blame them. So, let me clarify something on this matter.

    The fact that a singer may be able to sing a note doesn't mean they should. Once one has started voice lessons, their teacher will make sure they know this. Students will discover their "absolute range," which includes the highest and lowest pitch they can sing, and "viable range," the range in which they can appropriately and stylistically sing pitches. The "viable range" contains the pitches one can count on when indicating one's vocal range. Vocal fry, falsetto (for men), and whistle register should not be counted when determining range in classical singing.

    Although there are always exceptions, a common range for a well-trained classical male singer is about two and one-half octaves, and for a well-trained classical female approximately three octaves. Although some high coloraturas occasionally use "whistle register," this is rare and usually not counted in determining the vocal range.

Vocal Registers

The term "vocal register" was originally used by organists to describe different "stop" combinations used on the organ. Since the human voice made similar sound variations, the term was naturally applied to the voice. But today it is generally agreed that the voice is more like a double-reed wind instrument with the vocal cords on top of the trachea, supplied with air from the lungs.

Although there is some discrepancy over how many registers the singing voice has (some say up to five), in my opinion there are two true register differences in both male (full/chest and falsetto) and female (chest and head) singers, and three registers if you include the middle area of the voice where the lower and higher voices mix (mixed or middle register). Although some beginning students have learned to manipulate this precarious area (also known as the *passaggio*) of the voice naturally, unless the student has had some early guidance in how to approach the transition they have usually developed a definite "break" between the chest and head voice registers (full/chest voice and falsetto in men), which cannot be ignored and will have to be worked out with their voice teacher. The *passaggio* is explained in more detail later in this chapter.

Modal Voice

This area, which lies between vocal fry (the lowest, gravely sounding tones) and the whistle register (higher than the head voice or falsetto registers), is the most used in both speech and singing. It has a range of about two and a half octaves in well-trained male classical singers, and three octaves in well-trained female classical singers. Because there is a change between different muscle groups as the singer sings higher and higher within the modal voice, I have categorized the modal voice into different registers below. The area of *passaggio* (*zona di passaggio*) starts a perfect fifth to minor third below the top note of each of these registers and should mix seamlessly into the next register. See Figure 2 as a guide to the names of the notes in these ranges.

Female Registers

Chest Voice. The lowest register (above vocal fry) in the female voice types. The thyroarytenoid muscles are prominently in use. The chest register typically found in female voices is as follows (C4 = Middle C):

- Soprano: G3 to Eb4
- Mezzo-soprano: E3 to F4
- Contralto: C3 to C4

(The *primo passaggio* connects the chest register to the middle voice register at this point.)

Middle Voice. This normal speech or middle of the vocal range is where both chest and head voice are mixed and where both muscle groups, the thyroarytenoid and cricothyroid, are balanced and working together equally. The middle voice is found as follows:

- Soprano: Eb4 to F#5
- Mezzo-soprano: C4 to E5
- Contralto: A3 to G4

(The *secondo passaggio* connects the middle voice register to the head voice register at this point.)

Head Voice. (Also known as the loft register.) The highest register in a female singer just below the whistle register. The thyroarytenoid muscles are released and the cricothyroid muscles take over. The head voice register is found as follows:

- Soprano: F#5 to C#6
- Mezzo-soprano: E5 to B5
- Contralto: G4 to E5

Male Registers

Chest. (Also called low or full voice.) Equivalent to the female chest and middle voice. Both muscle groups, the thyroarytenoid and cricothyroid, are balanced and working together equally. However, on the lower end of this range the thyroarytenoid muscles are more in use, and on the upper part of this range of a well-trained classical singer there is a "mixing" of the full voice with the falsetto, causing the cricothyroid muscles to come more into play. The chest register typically appears in male voices as follows:

- Tenor: A2–D5
- Baritone: G2–Ab4
- Bass-baritone: E2–G4.
- Bass: D2–F4

(The *zona di passaggio* connects and mixes the chest voice and falsetto at this point.)

Falsetto. (Also known as the loft register.) The male equivalent to the female head voice. Falsetto functions as the thyroarytenoid muscles of the larynx starts working together with the cricothyroid muscles through the *passaggio*. These cricothyroids then take primary control in the falsetto register. Falsetto is not used when singing bass, bass-baritone, baritone, and tenor classical repertoire. The one exception would include high tenors who have chosen to develop the falsetto to sing countertenor repertoire.

Male countertenors, as well as pop, jazz, and rock singers, have learned to build up their falsetto to where it can be counted as part of their "viable range," allowing them to sing stylistically and with control up to an octave higher than the two-and-a-half-octave range used by classical singers.

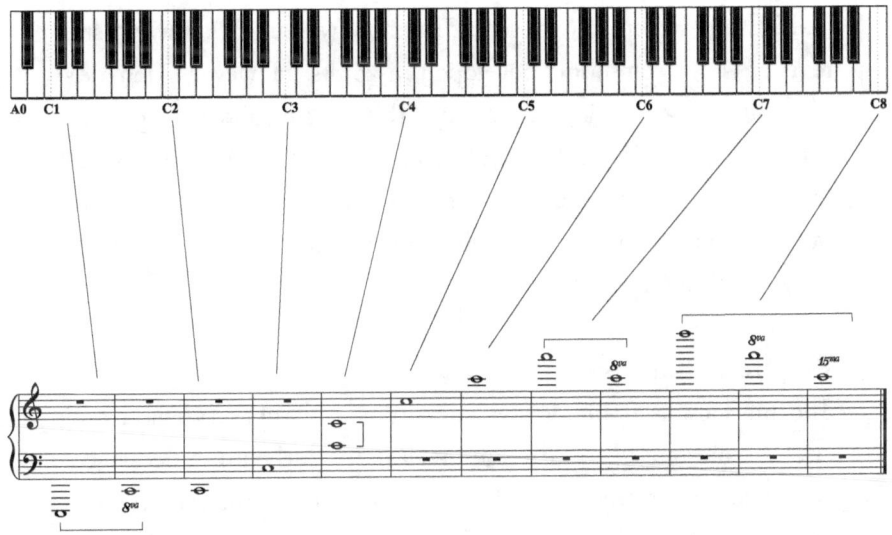

Figure 2. Keyboard reference for vocal ranges. (Source: John Ellinger).

Other Registers: Vocal Fry and Whistle

Vocal fry (also known as "glottal fry," "pulse register," or "strohbass") is achieved by either males or females when the singer frees the vocal folds of all tension, causing increased mass and reduced stretch, accounting for the production of the low fundamental frequency of 25 to 80 Hz in men and 20 to 45 Hz in women. This register is called glottal fry because of its sputtery, gravelly sound similar to that of something frying in a hot pan.

The whistle register (also called the "flageolet" or "flute" register) lies higher than the head voice of the female and the falsetto of the male and produces whistle- or flute-like notes up to two octaves above the modal voice. It is vocalized by air passing between the arytenoid cartilages through a triangular opening. Although sometimes used on quick successive notes by high coloratura sopranos, the whistle register is primarily used in contemporary popular music. Two pop singers famous for using this register include Mariah Carey and Minnie Riperton (whose highest note was an F7). The whistle register is not commonly developed in adults. However, a female's high-pitched scream is an example of this register, and some parents can attest to small children and babies having no problem producing pitches reaching even higher than those on the piano. It is most rare in the adult male voice and the least understood, physiologically, of all the registers.

Register Transition

The muscles used in register transition, the thyroarytenoid and cricothyroid muscle groups, are involuntary to the untrained voice. But once trained, the singer should be able to use these muscles to mix the registers, causing an even transition between them. This transition should then come naturally if there is:

1. Sufficient management of the breath.
2. A properly aligned vocal tract (lowered larynx and lifted soft palate).
3. Good posture or body alignment.
4. Forward placement of sensations in the mask.
5. Good engagement of the articulators.

Passaggio

The register transition, or *passaggio* (*Italian*, passageway), refers to the point of the voice where one crosses from one register to another. Usually the width of a major third or so, the term is most commonly used in reference to the transition between the chest voice and head voice in women, and between chest (also called full) voice and falsetto in men's voices. Untrained singers often observe an obvious "break" in this area because of the inability to "mix" the higher with the lower register during this transition. A sign of technical vocal mastery is to smoothly negotiate the *passaggio* without loss of resonance, range, or flexibility. In other words, the ability to engage the thyroarytenoid and cricothyroid muscle groups in as seamlessly balanced a way as possible.

Although many women feel there are two different *passaggio* areas, one between chest and middle voice and another between middle and head voice, the lower one is by far the most prevalent. Here are the *primo passaggio* areas that cause singers the biggest problems.

- Soprano: between G4 and B4 (Higher *passaggio* starts around F#5)
- Mezzo: between F4 and A4 (Higher *passaggio* starts around E5)
- Tenor: between G4 and C5
- Baritone: between E4 and Ab4
- Bass: between C4 and F4

Open-throated glides and hums are helpful in smoothing out the "break" the singer may experience while transitioning through the *passaggio*.

Mixing the Registers

Since the beginning of the seventeenth century with the introduction of opera, voices that were able to sing this demanding music were in great demand. Opera houses all over Europe were producing Italian opera, but because the *bel canto* technique of mixing registers was not known by singers in other countries, England, Russia,

Germany, and to a lesser degree France had to import Italian singers to sing in their opera houses.

For example, a bass trained in England or Russia who was singing above a middle C4 would have to strain and push up to about an E4 before he would experience a considerable break in his *passaggio* (see next section) and then a switch into a very unsupported falsetto. Italian basses trained in the *bel canto* method, however, had learned from their Italian voice teachers the secret of how to mix falsetto into their full voice starting around a B3. By thinking low into their breath support as they ascended and lifting the soft palate, lowering the larynx, and opening their throats, they were able to counteract the natural inclination for the throat to clamp up as they reached for the top notes. The Italians had discovered how to mix falsetto into their full voice to extend their upper range by approximately a major third. This not only gave them better control and more balance through the registers, they were able to sing for much longer without getting tired. Also, for Italian women singers, the use of head voice mixing with chest voice made for a smooth transition through their middle range and *passaggio* into their head voice.

This register-mixing technique was a very well-guarded secret for almost two centuries and only taught in other countries after Italian singers, trained in the technique, started living in other countries and teaching students themselves. Italy continued to be the most highly regarded country in which to learn opera until the early to middle twentieth century, when New York City became the most well-respected place to train as a singer.

VOICE CLASSIFICATIONS

The Fach System
As a classical singer specializing in opera, you've already realized that being a soprano, for example, does not mean that your voice is

right for all soprano arias and operatic roles. Although the ranges for most soprano roles are similar, the flexibility, weight, timbre, and other characteristics needed for that role may not be suitable to your voice or body type. Because of that, around the middle of the nineteenth century German opera houses developed a helpful system of categorizing voice types to help with auditioning and casting singers in roles they are most capable of performing. Today it is still more prevalently used in Europe but often used all over the world. In the Fach (German for "compartment") system, a singer's voice is classified using the following characteristics:

1. Size: How much sound is produced and how dramatic the voice is.
2. Range: How high and how low the voice can go.
3. Voice weight: How heavy, dark, agile, or light the voice is.
4. Timbre: The color, texture, and unique quality of the voice.
5. Tessitura: The place in a singer's range where it is most comfortable to sing.
6. Physical Characteristics: Age, build, and height.

I encourage every student of opera in the United States to take the Fach system seriously. Determine early in your career, with the help of your teacher, which category (Fächer) you are most likely to be cast in. Of course, as the voice develops this may change. But if you can figure out early where your voice lies and concentrate primarily on the arias that are most appropriate for you, it will save you much time and effort in avoiding singing repertoire from roles you will never be cast in.

I learned this the hard way after years of singing inappropriate arias at auditions and putting a mixture of roles on my resume. For some time I had no idea whether I was a basso profundo, basso cantabile, bass-baritone, or Verdi baritone, and it reflected on my resume. I had the range for all the low roles, so I just auditioned with arias I enjoyed learning. I figured having a good technique and command of the languages were the most important things. But musical directors don't want to THINK about your voice type when they're casting—they want to KNOW. They don't have the time to figure out your voice in a ten-minute audition ("He sounded great on the Falstaff aria, so why is he singing "In Diesen Heil'gen Hallen"?). My confusion confused them, and there were plenty of other auditionees who weren't confused. Only years later, when running my own concert opera company and sitting on the other side of the audition table, did I realize how many voice auditions I may have thrown away by not being clear about my Fach. Even though American opera houses do give more leeway in casting voices crossing over the line, you and your teacher should really put some time into narrowing down the five arias that best represent your voice before getting out there to audition.

Below you will find a list of voice types, their Fächer, and their ranges. I have not included the vocal qualities and body types needed for each voice category, nor have I included the roles that are historically most represented in each category. This would have taken many more pages. The serious singer should, nevertheless, research the Fach system and choose their repertoire accordingly.

Soprano: Lyric Coloratura C4-F6, Dramatic Coloratura C4-F6, Soubrette C4-C6, Lyric B3-C6, Spinto C4-C6, Dramatic B3-C6, Wagnerian F3-C6

Mezzo Soprano: Coloratura G3-B5, Lyric G3-B5, Dramatic G3-B5

Contralto: Dramatic F3-A5, Low E3-E5

Countertenor: G3–D5

Tenor: Lyric Comic (Buffo) C3–B4, Character B2–B4, Lyric C3–C5, Spinto C3–C5, Dramatic (Heroic/Heldentenor) C3–B4

Baritone: Light C3–B4, Lyric B2–Ab4, Cavalier A2–Ab4, Verdi A2–Ab4, Dramatic (Heldenbaritone) G2–F#4

Bass-baritone: Lyric E2–F4, Dramatic E2–F4

Bass: Comic (Buffo) C2–F4, Low (Basso Cantabile) C2–F4, Dramatic Low (Basso Profundo) C2–F4

"If you faithfully do your daily practice, without anxiety about the result, you will find yourself competent in the end." —LAMPERTI

HOW TO PRACTICE

Practice is the repetition of an action with the goal of improving that action. Effective practice not only takes time, but also depends on the quality of the practice, which should be consistent and well focused and which targets deficiencies and weaknesses that lay on the edge of the singer's current abilities.

How Practice Works

Imagine that a beginning vocal student has decided to work on a particular singing technique during a practice session. He or she thinks of the action, which activates the brain's gray matter (area of the brain that processes functions such as hearing, seeing, memory, and muscle control), which then sends the message down the spinal cord to a network of nerve fibers called axons, and then to the muscles. A fatty substance called myelin, a protective cover/insulation that surrounds the axons, starts to gradually get thicker with continued repetition of the same thought process. This thickened myelin covering helps prevent energy loss of the electrical impulses that the brain uses and sends the messages more efficiently along the neuro pathways of the axons. Studies suggest that continued repetition builds up layers of myelin around the axons, essentially creating the "hard wiring" needed to perfect a specific movement or action (Kirkwood, 2015).

If the singer doesn't perform a certain technique consistently, he or she will either take much longer in their development and/or develop poor singing habits. This is the main reason for taking voice lessons with an experienced and reputable teacher. A good teacher not only instructs the student in the correct way to sing but is also there to immediately evaluate and tweak incorrect technique to help the student keep their brain's message on the correct neurological pathway. This develops the muscle memory to a point where the appropriate action (technique) can be completed without conscious thought of how it's being done.

Below you will find the steps to effective vocal practice.

A. Set the scene

1. Find a quiet area of the house or school practice room, go in, and lock the door. Sorry, no friends allowed during the designated practice time.
2, Shut off all phones, social media, and texting applications. You don't need the distraction. Concentrating on the subject matter with no interruptions is important.
3. Make sure you have adequate lighting, a bottle of water, the required repertoire, and any items needed during your

practice (i.e., a piano, a recording/playing device, metronome, note pad, pencil, etc.).
4. Have a game plan. Know what you're going to practice and how long you want to spend on each aspect. Whether it be memorizing a song's text, mirror work, singing scales, or working on a certain technical aspect of a piece, practice time is much more effective when you aren't just practicing willy-nilly, working on whatever pops into your head.

B. *Warm up*

1. Total body warm-up: This would include some of the exercises we talked about earlier in this book on how to relax the jaw, tongue, shoulders, and neck as well as stretching the entire body. A tense instrument is an out-of-balance instrument!
2. Vocal warm-up/Working technique: How much time it takes to warm up depends on how much you've been singing lately. If you're singing a couple of hours a day, the warm-up time may only be ten minutes or so. If you haven't been singing much, you should warm up for at least a good twenty minutes. Scales, glides, and arpeggios are necessary to build muscle memory. Start each exercise slowly at first and then build up speed. Make sure to relax for a moment once in a while so there is no strain. I also find that certain phrases from arias or an art song work well as vocalises and make warm-up more interesting.

C. *Work on repertoire*

Throughout this book I've walked the reader through ways to work on all aspects of repertoire preparation. Refamiliarize yourself with these before working on the steps below:

1. Text Preparation
2. Rhythm Preparation
3. Note Preparation
4. Storyline Research
5. Stage Presence

D. Cool Down

After the practice period, do some nice relaxing glides and lip trills to warm down the voice.

"Those pupils who lack the patience to sing exercises exclusively for a few months will never become singers. Those who find exercises tiresome and sing do, re, me, without interest lack talent—but pupils who find beauty in all melodies have talent." —LAMPERTI

How Much Practice?

Most top musicians, dancers, and athletes spend fifty or more hours per week on things related to their instruments and split up daily practice sessions (more effective than one long session). I've often heard the formula that 10,000 hours of practice makes you an expert on anything you do. That's about ten years of three hours of practice a day, which sounds correct to me.

Beginning singing students, however, should start out with at least a half hour of practice every day. And it's more effective to break this half hour into two sessions of fifteen minutes. Practicing the exercises (vocalises) the teacher has assigned every day is critical for the vocal muscles and entire vocal instrument to remember how to coordinate and work together. Repetition equals muscle memory. The further the time between practice sessions, the harder it is for those muscles to remember. I look at beginning vocal instruction much like learning a new software. If you work with the software every day it won't be that long before you can go without referring back to the manual.

Practice length should be extended by the end of the first month and will start to include repertoire as soon as the teacher has determined the student has developed a reasonable amount of technique. Most young students sing in choirs and musicals in their high schools. This should not be used in lieu of their individual practice time. The beginner is trying to build correct technique and has to concentrate on the technical objectives set by their voice teacher, so choir is sometimes a distraction to the student's focus. Students have more time to concentrate on practice and solo repertoire during the summers, so individual voice lessons during these months are highly recommended. With this extra time to concentrate on their individual vocal technique, the student will eventually integrate what they learn into their choral singing.

Too Sick to Practice? Probably Not.

Everyone gets sick once in a while. Of course, if the student has a fever, they should get bed rest and not sing. However, if it's only a cold or even a sore throat, there are many practice regimens that can be accomplished without singing. There's really no excuse for not practicing (or coming to a lesson) if the student isn't contagious or doesn't have a fever.

Most practice can be done in the student's head or quietly mouthed:

1. If the student has built up a fairly good technique, they can look at the song and imagine they are singing the piece with correct inflections, tempo changes, stresses, and emotion.
2. If the song is in a foreign language they can, in their mind, concentrate on the meaning and definition of the text.

3. Memorization can always be done without opening the mouth.
4. Vocal technique and repertoire can be observed by watching great singers perform on YouTube. Watch where and how they breathe, their emotional phrasing, and text interpretation.
5. Listen to past recorded voice lessons and mark down in a journal what to work on and goals/objectives you want to achieve. Make a rehearsal game plan for the week!
6. Rhythm can be practiced in the head.
7. Researching the history and story line of the text is an essential part of practice. Why did the lyricist write those dreary or upbeat words? What was in the mind of the composer when he wrote the composition? Much of this information can be found online and in biographies.
8. There are hundreds of masterclasses given by great teachers and singers online. Also, many technical aspects of singing are covered by numerous online YouTube videos and vocal magazines. I have included the URLs to many of the most informative vocal online sites in Appendix II of this book.

VOCAL HEALTH DOS AND DON'TS

Singing takes a lot of healthy maintenance. The following guidance will help you make good decisions about your lifestyle as a singer and artist.

Dos

1. Hydrate. Drink plenty of water, about eight glasses each day, and always carry a bottle of water with you. Also, live in a place that has at least 40 percent humidity if you can. Use a vaporizer if your environment is dry.

2. Eat nutritious foods.
3. Get enough sleep, about 7–8 hours a night.
4. Use correct vocal technique to speak and sing (and yell).
5. During epidemics and flu season, wash your hands often, wear a mask, and social-distance with people who may be contagious.
6. Wear clothes appropriate to the temperature, which means covering up in cold weather. You may feel invincible when you're younger, but you're not! Stay dry and warm.
7. Warm up the voice before singing or speaking. Sirens and lip trills are good.
8. Warm down after a strenuous rehearsal. Glides and lip trills are good for this, too.
9. Practice carefully and as efficiently as possible.
10. Speak at your voice's optimal pitch. Speaking too low and the use of vocal fry are very damaging to the voice.

Don'ts

1. Avoid contagious people. If a person is sick, wait for three days before interacting with them. That's the usual incubation time before not being contagious. If there is no avoiding them, wear a face mask or teach online.
2. Seriously consider what you put into your body. Alcohol, drugs, tobacco, and caffeine in excess are a no-no. Also, it's possible that some antihistamines and other cold or allergy remedies may have a negative effect on the voice.
3. Don't talk too loud or scream, especially if the voice is tired. If the voice is sick or overworked, refuse to overuse your voice either professionally or personally. If talking is unavoidable, however, use the diaphragm and not the throat to support the sound.
4. Try to avoid as much stress as possible.

5. Do not use explosive glottal starts to words and phrases when speaking. This is very damaging to the vocal folds. Try speaking in a more legato style and at a higher pitch.
6. Avoid whispering. Use a well-supported *sotto voce* instead.
7. Avoid crying on a performance day. This causes muscular tension and sinus clogging.
8. Avoid vocal fry! Be conscious how you end your sentences. Support your speaking voice all the way through the sentence and don't "fry out" at the end.

ADDRESSING COMMON VOCAL PROBLEMS

Vibrato Imbalance

These three irregular vibrato patterns are a result of a malfunctioning vocal process that includes three factors, either by themselves or in combination:

1. Hypo-functional (too slow) or hyper-functional (too fast) muscular activity.
2. Emotional state such as depression or excitement.
3. Physical conditions such as vocal fold injury, tension, fatigue, or nervous disorder.

Wobble

The most effective way of fixing wobble (vibrato rate of less than 5.5 oscillations per second), particularly with older choir singers, is to practice singing more than three times a week and having a normal exercise regimen. Singing regularly tones up the vocal muscles and physical exercise helps with muscle tone, support muscles, and posture. A strong voice deteriorates over the years from nonuse or sickness.

However, successful, long-careered singers may also develop a wobble in their later years. This is usually accompanied by poor intonation. Little can be done about "overuse syndrome," the result of an overuse of the voice over countless years at highly intensive levels, under sometimes less than adequate working conditions.

Tremolo

The tremolo has a rapid vibrato rate of more than 7.5 oscillations per second and is the result of tension and unbalanced breath support.

If this is the case, the singer must relax the throat and breathe low. Humming and lip trills are often effective in stabilizing the larynx and bringing the breath support back into balance, which establishes a continuous phonation.

A singer with this problem should work with a good voice teacher and relearn this essential aspect of breath support. Somehow the singer has either never learned or has over the years redeveloped the bad habit of breathing high, which left the voice unbalanced and full of tension and pressure, causing an increase in the rate of vibrato. Stage fright can also cause excitement and tension, which may bring on a rapid vibrato rate. I will discuss how to fix this later in this chapter.

Straight Tone

Straight tone is often difficult to completely eliminate. But unless it is intentionally being used as an effect or vocal styling, it's a sign of laryngeal tension caused by not knowing correct vocal technique or deliberate holding of the larynx. The latter is often the result of singing in straight-tone choirs that attempt to imitate the sound made by a boys' choir or an early music style. See "Bad Choral Habits" later in this chapter. The student may also be singing and belting musical theater or other contemporary styles such as pop or R&B. Switching back and forth from classical singing to these styles often confuses students and their ability to sing a normal vibrato when needed.

To relax the throat enough to allow a natural vibrato means low breathing and a balanced flow of air. However, to manually kick-start the process of vibrato I highly suggest practicing a technique I use to develop the trill. Alternating between two half steps, gradually get faster until there is an even shake between the two half steps. After the throat has relaxed enough to alternate between the two notes (use a metronome if that helps), start supporting with a low, solid breath and observe how wide and fast the shake is. If it's too much, give it a touch of the straight tone until the vibrato is modified to a pleasant width and speed.

Scooping

This bad vocal habit slurs a lower note to a higher note. Unlike a conscious musical effect such as a *portamento*, scooping may be caused by several factors, such as an adjustment after singing a wrong pitch, imitation of another singer's stylistic musicality, or an imbalanced registration caused by age or misuse. Conscious work on scale intervals and leaps while always maintaining a forward breath momentum will help correct this problem. If you're taking lessons your teacher has certainly heard them and should work on this problem with you. Record your practice to hear where you are scooping and mark your score to remind you to pay attention and avoid it.

Poor Choral Habits

When accepting new students, I always ask if they've done much choral singing. If the answer is yes, I naturally assume that this is a good thing and should be beneficial in training the voice during individual study. However, I sometimes find that this isn't the case at all. Unless they've learned good technique from their choir directors, it's almost better that the student has no choral background.

It's easier to start with a clean slate than to fix all the vocal problems caused by a choir director who has taught poor vocal technique. If the director hasn't taken an adequate amount of private study themselves, developing bad vocal habits aren't recognized in rehearsal by the director and corrected quickly enough. These bad habits must then be addressed in private voice lessons if the student is to improve.

I won't rehash the fixes for these bad habits, as I've already given them throughout the book. I just want to point out the importance that choral directors should also be well-trained singers who continually monitor their students' individual development and not just the choral sound as a whole.

Here are a few of the most common bad choral habits that tend to slow down the progress of young singers (also lowering the effectiveness of the choir's sound). All of these can be fixed, with the assistance of a proficient teacher, if the student is open-minded to change and willing to reject poor vocal habits that have previously been built into their muscle memory during their time in choir.

1. Breathy tone
2. Poor vowel formation
3. Poor breathing techniques: too much, too soon, and too little
4. Lack of a balanced vibrato
5. Poor posture

Stage Fright

Performance anxiety, or stage fright, is often the result of a traumatic childhood experience while performing or getting in front of an audience for the first time. As I mentioned in an earlier chapter, for me it was at my first piano recital. After a mix-up of when I was supposed to play, I had made a mistake big enough that I had to start over. My mother was sitting in the audience right behind me and when I made the mistake, she "tsked" me. Needless to say, I fell apart and ruined the rest of the performance. For years after that I was afraid to get up in front of an audience.

Although I still have some nerves before performing (a small amount is good), positive performing experiences throughout my life have relieved that anxiety. Here are a few things that helped me cope with performance anxiety.

Relaxation and Positive Thinking: Some techniques to help muscle tension release and calm the mind are yoga, meditation, hypnosis, and biofeedback. When in a relaxed state of mind, imagine the upcoming performance in which your voice feels and sounds beautiful; hear how the crowd claps enthusiastically afterward; feel their handshakes as they come up to congratulate you for a job well done after the performance. Feel the joy and satisfaction of your achievement. Really feel as if you are there and know that it is so.

Being well prepared: Performers who know they have prepared well, are confident about all the words and notes, and are technically proficient will be much less anxious before and while performing. They'll know that they've chosen appropriate repertoire and have practiced enough that their cognitive and muscle memory will do their part.

Beta blockers: Although I don't recommend using these, some singers turn to them to reduce tremors and help control the heart rate. Talk with your doctor about using them, especially if you have asthma or some kind of cardiac disease. Also, research natural food and vitamin substitutes that may have a calming effect. Certain scents sometimes work.

Low, deep breaths: One of the most effective calming steps I take just before going onstage is taking slow, low, and deep breaths for about five minutes. It does wonders in slowing down the heart rate and gets the singer breathing low and in the correct place for singing.

SUMMARY

I've covered a lot of information in these six chapters and I truly thank you for sticking with it to the end! Ten years ago, I started to write down ideas for my students to work on at home, and since then I have been gathering those together with research papers I've written and notes on my reading and instruction gleaned from teachers and coaches. If anything in this book is new to you or has caused you to rethink your approach, if any of the exercises and fixes have worked in improving your voice, if what I've expounded on in these pages has kept you engaged and hasn't put you to sleep, I've done my job!

Finishing this book in 2020 during the Covid-19 pandemic has been a time of isolation from students, friends, and family. While this has been a productive time for writing, it has also been a period of hardship and loss for many, including performers and artists of all kinds who have faced closed theaters and opera houses. But through it all, we have had the beauty of music to fall back on. We have held to the hope that the arts will flourish again when this crisis passes. And we cherish, more than ever, the singers who internalize and then share with the world the vibration and resonant beauty that lies within, expressed through beautiful singing.

APPENDIX I

Vocal Disorders and Faults

"Difficulties in singing come from three directions: uneducated hearing, undisciplined muscles and untrained breathing."
—Lamperti

There are many bumps in the road in the professional singer's life. When these challenges involve illnesses or disorders that negatively affect vocal technique and the production of the resonance that the singer has worked so hard to achieve, it can be devastating.

Singers are not the only people who suffer from vocal disorders. Anyone who uses their voice to carry out their job can be referred to as a "professional" or "athletic" voice user. These include singers, actors, voice-over talent, teachers, clergy, athletic coaches, voice teachers, salespersons, auctioneers, cheerleaders, and broadcasters. According to the Merck Manual (2020), the most common ailments affecting these professionals are not serious and can be treated by vocal rest, learning techniques (like *bel canto*!) to avoid abusing the voice, proper hydration, and taking medication for acid reflux. In general, Clarence T. Sasaki (2020) in the Merck Manual states:

> *People who use their voice professionally for public speaking and singing often experience voice disorders manifesting as hoarseness or breathiness, lowered vocal pitch, vocal fatigue, nonproductive cough,*

persistent throat clearing, and/or throat ache. These symptoms often have benign causes, such as vocal nodules, vocal fold edema, polyps, or granulomas. Such disorders are usually caused by vocal fold hyperfunction (excessive laryngeal muscular tension when speaking) and possibly gastroesophageal reflux.

In this appendix I explain some of the most common ailments and more serious conditions that singers and professional voice athletes may experience, the types of doctors they use when something goes wrong, and some of the analysis instruments used to register and record vocal manipulation of the larynx. My sources come from an array of books and websites.

COMMON VOCAL DISORDERS

Acid Reflux (Laryngopharyngeal Reflux-LPR). When it comes to singers, acid reflux can have a devastating effect. Stomach acid backs up the throat and burns the vocal folds, causing hoarseness and laryngitis.

Although there is an extreme type that causes heartburn (GERD, Gastroesophageal Reflux Disease) there is a much more silent type of GERD that often damages the vocal folds without the singer knowing it. According to Witten at the Boston Singers Resource (2020), symptoms for this type of GERD include the need to clear the throat, feeling a lump in the throat, a cough that won't go away, difficulty swallowing, and a mild hoarseness of the throat.

Ways to prevent acid reflux include reducing alcohol and coffee consumption, eating less spicy foods, not eating before going to sleep, eating smaller meals (especially before a performance), using prescription or over-the-counter antacids, elevating the head two to six inches when sleeping, avoiding stress, losing weight, and not exercising right after a meal.

Adenoids. Glands that trap germs coming into the mouth and nose and produce white blood cell antibodies to help stop infections. Located where the nose meets the throat and behind the soft palate, they often disappear by the time one reaches adulthood. When the adenoids become infected, it may turn into a condition called *adenoiditis*. Symptoms include speaking with a nasal sound, sore throat, ear pain, swollen glands, or difficulty sleeping (WebMD, 2020).

Aging. Signs most associated with aging singers include increased breathiness, erratic hydration, loss of lung elasticity and the effects of muscle atrophy, decreased coordination, blood flow, and memory loss/concentration. Some of the changes of the larynx are due to it turning to bone (ossification and calcification). Low hormone levels such as with women's estrogen during menopause and men's testosterone tend to lower female voices and raise men's voices.

The weakening of the vocal folds, which causes the voice to be wobblier and the vocal folds flabby, can sometimes be surgically altered in a voice augmentation process called a "voice lift" or *laryngoplasty*. For those voice professionals who feel they need help, two different voice lift procedures can help tighten the vocal cords and deal with other age-related changes. An injection *laryngoplasty* uses injectable fillers much like those used for lips and to tighten facial wrinkles. The other, called a *medialization laryngoplasty*, uses tiny implants made out of Gore-Tex or silicon to help tighten up the vocal folds. Of course, even though both procedures are becoming commonplace, they should be researched and taken seriously before altering something as fragile as the vocal folds (Breslow, 2017).

Ankyloglossia. This is when the membrane connecting the tongue to the mouth's floor (frenulum) decreases the tongue's mobility ("tongue-tied"), affecting singing, eating, and speech. If the singer looks under the tongue, they will notice this membrane. Those with ankyloglossia often have it connected all the way to the tip of the tongue or tightly connected from the floor of the mouth to the underside of the tongue. This condition often causes speech disorders and lessens the rate and range of articulation, which can be very restrictive to a singer. The most common way to fix this is to have surgery (*lingual frenulectomy*) to cut back and relieve the restrictive effect of the attached frenulum. This is done by the doctor in an outpatient procedure either with a scalpel or a soft-tissue laser (Morrison, 2017).

Asthma. There are approximately eight million asthma sufferers living in the United States, and while most attacks are triggered by allergies, exercising, exposure to cold air, certain drugs, and stress may also trigger attacks. Shortness of breath, throat clearing, dry coughs, and wheezing are a few asthmatic symptoms. There is no cure to asthma, but there are helpful medications. On the American Academy of Allergy, Asthma and Immunology website, Murphy (2020) has created a reference to commonly used medications for asthma.

Bronchitis. Along with a fever, bronchitis symptoms are similar to asthma, and the illness is often caused by viruses that cause the common cold. They're triggered by irritant particles (of which smoke is one) causing an inflammation of the bronchial tubes that cause symptom such as headache, blocked nose and sinuses, sore throat, tightness in the chest, low fever, and a mucus-producing cough. If an infection occurs, it may be treated with ibuprofen, lots of fluids, cough medicine, use of a humidifier, and a good amount of rest. Acute bronchitis may last only a couple of days, but chronic bronchitis may last for years and can flare into more dangerous respiratory diseases such as emphysema or pneumonia (McIntosh, 2019).

Deviated Septum. When the cartilage that separates the nostrils of the nose (septum) is out of place, there is more likelihood for sinus infections and nasal congestion. Headaches, nosebleeds, snoring, and difficulty of breathing through the nose are other signs the singer may have a deviated septum. This condition is often present at birth but can be caused by an injury to the nose. In lesser cases medication may help, but often it takes getting a "nose job" (*septoplasty*) to straighten and reconstruct the septum so there is no obstruction (Gabbey and Gotter, 2019).

Hypothyroidism. "A condition in which the thyroid gland cannot produce a sufficient volume of thyroid hormone. Thyroid hormones affect every cell in the body which is why you are likely to experience signs and symptoms that affect your overall health as opposed to one set of localized symptoms." Low thyroid function causes range loss, a hoarse or sore throat, vocal fatigue, muffled sound, hoarseness, and the feeling there is a lump in the throat (Kingston, 2019).

Hydration. Drinking enough water keeps the singer's vocal cords limber, helps their cells communicate more effectively, and maintains equilibrium in the nervous system. Although a sip of water helps to lubricate the throat, to be truly effective water must go through the whole body to lubricate the entire larynx and vocal cords. Drinking a regular bottle of water at least an hour before singing is best. Hydration also helps to heal and prevent illness.

Stage environment, airplanes, air-conditioning, and the energy spent on the physical performance of singing takes a high intake of water. Drinking six to eight 16-ounce containers of water a day on average is a good habit. Also, the use of a portable humidifier is highly recommended for the traveling singer to help keep nasal passages moist.

Irritable Larynx Syndrome (ILS). This is basically an irritation of the mucosa of the larynx that causes symptoms that are not related to a specific disease. Besides dry and thick secretions, symptoms include throat burning or irritation, chronic cough, throat tightness, throat clearing, and spasm of the larynx. Irritants that bring on these symptoms include hair spray, perfume, cigarette smoke, allergens, acid reflux, cold air, strong emotions such as stress, and fumes from harsh chemicals (Michael, 2020).

Leukoplakia. A condition that causes thick white patches on the tongue and other parts of the mouth. White patches in the mouth are usually temporary and painless, but when they persist these long-lasting lesions may be a signal that they have developed into leukoplakia, signaling possible oral cancer and a need for required medical treatment (Cleveland Clinic, 2020).

Menopause. "Estrogen deprivation causes substantial changes in the mucous membranes that line the vocal tract. As estrogen levels decrease, laryngeal tissues begin to absorb water causing the vocal folds to swell, blood vessels to become enlarged, and vocal fold mass to increase." Registration imbalance causes a bigger break between the chest and head voice and the voice becomes pushed. The singer may feel a thickness in the throat and develop a vocal wobble due to laryngeal muscle tension. High range begins to suffer (Swanson, 2018).

Menstruation. During this time, the voice tires more easily and may become hoarse. The vocal folds are thick due to increased water and blood to the muscles and tissues of the throat due to an increase in antidiuretic hormone and altered progesterone and estrogen levels associated with changes. In addition, cramps may affect breath support. "Premenstrual vocal syndrome includes the loss of vocal power, range and harmonics, and a reduced ability to sing pianissimo. Also, drier vocal cords during menstruation make it more difficult to control vibrato" (Chandler, 2018). Diuretics should never be used by singers in their premenstrual period.

Performance Anxiety (Stage Fright). When a singer experiences stage fright, Sarah Cosgrove (2005) explains, "The degree of distress or of the perceived threat will affect the intensity of physical response . . . and activates the amygdala (in the brain) which in turn activates: (1) Arousal systems within the brain, (2) Sympathetic division of the autonomic nervous system." This can constrict the throat and play havoc with the singer's tone quality. As I explained in Chapter six, a few ways to ease stage fright are: 1. Relaxation and Positive Thinking 2. Being Well Prepared 3. Low, Deep Breaths, and 4. Beta Blockers if need be.

Pregnancy. The effects on the singing voice caused by pregnancy include morning sickness, exhaustion, trouble swallowing, hoarseness caused by postnasal drip (brought on by hormones and called *pregnancy rhinitis*), and a drying out of the vocal fold cover (*mucosa*). Abdominal muscles lose tone from a stretched stomach (*diastasis recti*), which weakens the balance of the core muscles affecting breathing. After delivery singers can work through some of these conditions by keeping up daily voice training. "Binding of the abdomen from below the pubic bone to just below the sternum within the first day or two after giving birth, then continuing to bind twenty-four hours a day for a few months after delivery may help to draw these muscles closer, and will stabilize the pelvis and the lower back (which are dependent on the strength and alignment of the abdominal muscles to provide good postural support)" (O'Conner, 2020).

Sinus infections, Colds, and Allergies. When the sinus passages are full of mucus, the tiny holes in them are blocked and the pressure causes a sinus headache. This mucus also contains bacteria that can cause the entire vocal tract and respiratory system to become infected. A clogged nose from a sinus infection or cold does little to affect the actual resonance, however, if the singer is using the correct technique, that of placing the voice forward in the mouth instead of back near the sinuses. Singers will not be able to hear themselves as well, but unless the infection causes the throat to swell or coughing hurts the vocal cords, singers are usually able to sing through these common ailments.

For prevention of sinus infections, the active singer should have a regimen for cleaning out the sinuses. A favorite of mine, and one used by many of my New York singer friends, is a mucus solvent called Alkalol ®. When used correctly, Neti Pots ®, saltwater irrigation devices, steamers, and inhalers are also very helpful for staying in good sinus health.

Spasmodic Dysphonia. This is a disorder (found primarily in women between age 30 and 50) in which the muscles that operate the larynx spasm every so often, causing interruptions or breaks in the voice and making speech difficult to understand. Caused by a dysfunction in the basal ganglia or cerebral cortex, areas of the brain that coordinate muscle movement throughout the body, this voice disorder can only be diagnosed after an examination by a team of specialists, including and otolaryngologist, a speech-language pathologist, and a neurologist. There is currently no cure, but treatments include botulinum toxin injections, voice therapy, and surgery, when more conventional methods have failed (NIH, 2020).

TMJ Syndrome. This a condition in which the temporomandibular joint (where the jaw connects to the skull) does not function properly. There is often a catch or click in the joint when the mouth is extended wide open, which can cause pain in the jaw that can radiate to many other muscles of the neck, head and shoulders. Some causes include genetics, grinding of teeth, arthritis, habitual gum chewing, or an injury to the jaw. The ability to lower the jaw, and therefore larynx, may be hampered and the singer may find it difficult to achieve an adequate resonant space in the mouth, especially when singing classically.

This condition is far from unusual (actually one in four people have TMJ symptoms, with women being twice as likely) and I have often encountered students who find this problem a real source of irritation. Seeing how a loose jaw is essential in accessing lower breath support and a relaxed throat, this condition may keep a student from seriously pursuing a classical or operatic career. However, if the student enjoys singing musical theater or pop, and doesn't have a bad case of TMJ, they would find it much easier to maintain a space that doesn't have a need to lower the larynx and raise the soft palate as extremely as required in singing opera or classical music.

Treatment involves a complete evaluation of the bite with possible "bite splint therapy" being recommended to help stabilize the joint, keep the teeth apart, and "center the TMJ into its most stable position" (Otsego Dental, 2020).

Tone Deafness. The inability to distinguish the difference and relative space between musical notes. Although many people say they are tone deaf, it is a rare dysfunction, dealing with coordination between hearing and the physical response of singing a note in tune.

Tonsillitis. Tonsils are lymph nodes located on both sides of the back of the throat that function as a defense mechanism to prevent infection. If there is swelling of the tonsils due to a virus or bacterial infection a condition called tonsillitis is produced. This is a common problem primarily affecting children, though adults may contract it as well. The inflamed tonsils can cause a sore throat, fever, and trouble swallowing, while also causing an overly nasal sound (hyper nasality) and a restriction of tongue movement, causing distorted consonants and blocking nasal airflow. Plenty of rest and fluids for dehydration, the taking of acetaminophen or ibuprofen and throat lozenges, and a humidifier to moisten the air are all helpful in relieving the pain and discomfort of tonsillitis. If the infection is caused by bacteria it may result in an even more sever strep infection, where the doctor may prescribe antibiotics. Frequent infections of the tonsils may call for a *tonsillectomy*, an operation used to remove the tonsils (Pietrangelo, 2019).

Tonsil Stones. Hard particles that remain after white blood cells have attacked foreign objects on the tonsils are called tonsil stones. Gargling with salt water or rubbing the tonsils with a toothbrush or cotton swab can often remove them, but in some cases the more deeply embedded particles need to be removed by a doctor. A *tonsillectomy* is a last resort.

Trauma from Intubation. When anesthesia is used for surgery, an intubation tube is placed in the mouth, down through the larynx and between the vocal folds, and into the windpipe. This often causes irritation to the throat and bruising of the vocal folds that may affect the voice for months to follow. If a singer needs to undergo anesthesia for surgery, he or she should at first have a direct conversation with the surgeon and anesthesiologist about the procedure and request that the anesthesiologist use less irritating plastic rather than a rubber intubation tube. The patient should also ask the doctor to use the smallest circumference tube as possible. Also, "Because aspiration of stomach contents can occur, it is important that proton pump inhibitors are given pre and postoperatively to minimize complications from acid reflux."

Although most of the postoperative symptoms abate within seventy-two hours, the following weeks are important in the recovery, so the singer should not try to compensate for any vocal weaknesses using technique when starting up a singing routine. The singer should expect three to six months to fully recover before the singing voice is back to normal (Ragan, Gangopadhyay, 2012).

Viral Pharyngitis. This is the medical name for a sore throat caused by a viral infection such as the common cold or flu. A sore throat can cause a husky voice and bring on a fever and cough. Singers can find some relief by taking acetaminophen, gargling with salt water, drinking warm tea or lemon water, and taking throat lozenges.

DRUGS AND THEIR EFFECTS

Alcohol, sedatives, nicotine, muscle relaxants, and sedatives. All affect the muscles in the throat and prevent them from reacting precisely.

Analgesics. These pain-relieving medicines can be sold over the counter or by subscription. Over-the-counter, nonsteroidal anti-inflammatory drugs (NAIDs) such as aspirin, Motrin, Aleve, or Advil can contribute to vocal cord hemorrhage and tinnitus if the singer has enlarged blood vessels in their vocal cords and is then traumatized by excessive vocal use and should be avoided at all costs. Even ibuprofen, which interferes with blood clotting, should be avoided. Tylenol (which contains acetaminophen) is the best substitute for aspirin when singing.

Side effects of prescription analgesics (of which opioids are one) include dry mouth, dizziness, constipation, drowsiness, upset stomach, itchy skin, and ringing in the ears (Marks, 2015).

Anesthetics. These pain-relieving drugs are usually used in spray form to numb the affected area. (Example: Chloraseptic® spray, when sprayed in the back of the throat, will help to mask or alleviate the discomfort of a sore throat.) If the sore throat is severe though, the singer should cancel their rehearsal, practice, or performance if at all possible. Damage to the vocal cords may be caused if the pain is only masked and is sung on too strenuously.

Antibiotics. Also called an antibacterial, the first antibiotic, penicillin, was discovered in 1928. Antibiotics kill or keep bacteria from growing when fighting infections (Example: strep throat, some ear and sinus infections, whooping cough, dental infections) but cannot be used against problems caused by a virus such as upper-respiratory tract infections, flus, or colds (including the coronavirus). A couple of common names for modern antibiotics include amoxicillin and ampicillin. Side effects affect one in ten people and include a loss of appetite, abdominal pain, diarrhea, rash, swelling of the tongue and face, difficulty breathing, bloating and indigestion, nausea, and vomiting (Felman, 2019).

Antihistamines. This is usually the first medication when treating allergies such as hay fever, indoor, and food allergies. Caused by histamines, which cause stuffy noses, runny eyes, and itching, it is often taken with a decongestant. More difficult allergy problems may have to be treated by steroids or allergy shots. A few side effects are dizziness, dry mouth, restlessness, blurred vision, confusion, nausea, and trouble peeing (WebMD, 2019).

Corticosteroids. A synthetic anti-inflammatory drug used to reduce swelling and manage a variety of disorders such as asthma and acute inflammatory laryngitis. It is occasionally prescribed to the working singer by their laryngologist if the vocal folds are swollen and the performer absolutely has to be onstage. However, if the singer feels he or she needs them in order to overcome a weakened voice condition, they should cancel the performance rather than run the risk of permanently harming the vocal cords by singing on them too strenuously in an inflamed condition. More often steroids are given in low doses over longer lengths of time than higher doses over shorter periods of time. Some of the risks from using steroids are mood changes, vocal hemorrhage, dependency on steroids, worsening of a vocal injury, acne, and permanent weight gain from overuse. Anabolic steroids, known for their abuse by athletes, should never be used for voice treatment (Gupta, 2019).

VOCAL FOLD DISORDERS

Bogart-Bacall Syndrome. Named after Humphrey Bogart and Lauren Bacall, who were known for their naturally husky speaking voices. A voice disorder caused by the abuse or overuse of the vocal cords by people who speak and sing below their natural vocal range. More prevalent in women who want to sound more authoritative, some of the symptoms include hoarseness, unnaturally deep or rough voice, vocal fatigue, sore larynx, and loss of voice. Treatment may include speech therapy by a speech pathologist, vocal rest, hydration, breath training and medication (Medical Centric, 2018).

Contact Ulcers. These are red sores that develop on the mucous membrane of the arytenoid cartilage connecting the vocal fold, caused by abusive forceful speech using hard glottal attacks. A contact ulcer is also known as a *granuloma*. The typical treatment is an in-office medical procedure (Dhillon, 2020).

Cysts. Less common than nodules or polyps, these lesions are often developed when using the voice when sick with an upper respiratory infection or laryngitis (Dhillon, 2020).

Hemorrhage. Bleeding as a result of bruising and breaking of blood vessels in vocal folds caused by forcefully using the voice in an abusive way, and trauma from surgical intubation. This includes coughing, shouting, incorrect singing technique or aggressive singing style, and throat clearing. This bleeding in the cords may often turn into nodes or polyps (Dhillon, 2020).

Laryngeal Cancer. The symptoms of this rare cancer of the larynx, usually caused by smoking or alcohol use, include a hoarseness or cough that does not go away, pain when swallowing, a lump on the neck or throat, trouble making sounds or breathing, ear pain, or a feeling that there is something in the throat. Like other cancers, chemotherapy, radiation, and surgery are traditional treatments (Dhillon, 2020).

Nodules. When repetitive speaking or singing with poor vocal technique causes trauma to the vocal folds, they may swell. Over time these areas of swelling, caused by broken blood vessels, begin to harden and become growths or callouses called vocal fold nodules. These lesions, often called "nodes" for short, keep the folds from vibrating correctly and cause hoarseness, voice breaks, and a decreased vocal range. A pain in the neck or lump in the throat may be experienced. Vocal rest and occasionally surgery are needed to remove them, followed by voice lessons to rehabilitate and correct any problems that caused the nodes in the first place (Dhillon, 2020).

Polyps. This type of lesion on the vocal fold resembles a blister and is usually larger than a nodule and more reddish in color. Also caused by vocal trauma, sometimes in a single episode such as yelling, they can also be caused by smoking, alcohol, sinusitis, and allergies (Dhillon, 2020).

Vocal Cord Paralysis. "Paralysis of the vocal cords may happen when one or both vocal cords doesn't open or close properly. When one vocal cord is paralyzed, the voice can be weak or food or liquids can slip into the trachea and lungs, whereby people have trouble swallowing and may choke or cough when they eat. Patients with both vocal cords paralyzed may have trouble breathing. Vocal cord paralysis may be caused by the following: Head, neck, or chest injury, problem during surgery, stroke, tumor, lung or thyroid cancer, certain neurological disorders, such as multiple sclerosis or Parkinson's disease, and viral infection. Treatment may include surgery and voice therapy" (Dhillon, 2020).

Vocal Strain and Fatigue/Laryngitis. Caused by incorrect singing for long lengths of time (vocal dosing). Also, excessive speaking and yelling done by teachers, conductors, cheerleaders, and telephone solicitors can cause vocal fatigue, especially in noisy environments. Environment, dehydration, low thyroid function, and not enough sleep can also be major factors. To help avoid vocal strain one should always get seven to nine hours of sleep a night, be well hydrated, and warm up at least ten minutes before full-blown singing or professional speaking (Sutton, 2017).

TYPES OF DOCTORS FOR VOCAL AILMENTS

Allergist. Singers who develop hay fever, asthma, hive and skin allergies, or potentially fatal allergic reactions (anaphylaxis) need this type of physician. Once diagnosed, an allergist can offer immunotherapy, allergy shots, medications, and preventative education.

ENT (Ear, Nose and Throat doctor). Also called an otolaryngologist, an ENT can help with throat infections, ear infections, and sinus problems and specializes in treating diseases of the neck and head.

In a subspecialty of otolaryngology, a laryngologist is a physician who specializes in the larynx and vocal disorders such as nodes or polyps, swallowing, hoarseness, cancer, traumatic injury, reflux, and more. Also called a phono surgeon, phoniatrist, or voice doctor, they often work in a team that includes a speech language pathologist. Some of the instruments used to monitor and diagnose vocal disorders include the laryngoscope, electroglottograph (EGG), and vocal dosimeter. All of these instruments are described in the next section (Mayo Clinic, 2020).

Singing Voice Specialist. This professional voice teacher has special training allowing them to practice in a medical environment with patients who have sustained vocal injury. Most singing voice specialists have a degree in voice performance or pedagogy. . . . Nearly all have professional performance experience, as well as extra training in laryngeal anatomy and physiology of phonation, training in the rehabilitation of injured voices, and other special education. The singing voice specialist must acquire knowledge of anatomy and physiology of the normal and disordered voice, fundamental knowledge of the principles and practices of laryngology and medications, and a fundamental knowledge of the principles and practices of speech-language pathology (Sataloff, 2006).

SOFTWARE AND INSTRUMENTS FOR MEASURING THE VOICE

The use of computers and software to scientifically analyze the voice has had a large impact on our knowledge of the voice and how it functions. Not since Manuel Garcia discovered the laryngoscope in 1854 has the voice/science community learned so much about how the voice is created. Here are a few of the measuring and analytical software and devices used today.

Electroglottograph (EGG). An electronic device called a glottograph is placed on the side of the singer's neck and monitors the contact area between the two vocal folds by measuring the electrical resistance through the glottis while it is vibrating. The instrument then prints this record.

Laryngoscope. Instrument for examining the vocal cords. There are two types of examinations using this instrument. One, called a *direct fiberoptic laryngoscopy*, uses a small telescope at the end of a cable to go through the nose and into the throat. The second kind of examination is a *direct laryngoscopy*. This is a more involved procedure, with the laryngoscope pushing down the tongue, lifting up the epiglottis, and sending down a video camera to the larynx, where it can examine the vocal folds and anything else in the area. The first direct laryngoscopy was performed in 1895 by Alfred Kirstein of Germany. However, the famous voice teacher Manuel Garcia "also used the sun as an external light source to view the glottis using a tool he developed with two mirrors" (Pantano, 2015).

Nasometer™. This device incorporates two microphones mounted on either side of a plate that is placed between the upper lip and the nose of the subject to measure relative sound pressure escaping from the nose and acoustic output. It also measures speech articulation and nasality when speaking (nasalance) (Watterson, 2020).

See-scape™. This mechanical device is used to detect nasal emissions and measure nasal airflow during speech or singing while also confirming abnormal resonance.

Stroboscope. This instrument is used to perform "[a] special method of examination (*stroboscopy*) of a vibrating or fast-moving object, such as the vocal folds. A bright flashing light lasting a fraction of a second (10μs) is used to illuminate the vocal folds. This flash 'freezes' the movement of the vibrating vocal folds." More detailed and thorough than a laryngoscope (McGlashan, 2016).

Vocal Dosimeter. A portable digital recording device that uses small contact microphones attached right below the singer's Adam's apple to measure vocal fold elapsed phonation time and vocal intensity data.

VoceVista™. This is a voice analysis software that uses a spectrogram for real-time analysis of the voice through spectrum analysis, voice resonance analysis, and pitch detection. A spectrogram is used to get an idea of what is happening in the vocal tract and record the formant process for visual study. Nair (1999) states, "This is a three-dimensional graphic representation of the analysis of sound showing time on the horizontal axis, frequency on the vertical axis, and amplitude as intensity of color or grayscale."

Videofluoroscope. A flexible fiber optic scope and a video camera to go in through the nose and look at the vocal mechanism from above.

APPENDIX II

Internet Resources for Singers

ONLINE JOURNALS, MAGAZINES, AND ASSOCIATIONS

American Academy of Teachers of Singing (AATS)
"A select group of nationally recognized teachers of singing and voice experts. Members include those who are faculty at prestigious colleges, universities, and conservatories, as well as teachers in independent studios."
> http://www.americanacademyofteachersofsinging.org/index.php

Boston Singer's Resource
Singing links and resources.
> http://www.bostonsingersresource.com/resources/vocal-health/links-resources/

Classical Singer Magazine
Monthly magazine, interviews, vocal health tips, auditions.
> https://www.classicalsinger.com/

CS Music
Articles, auditions, events, competitions, directories
> https://www.csmusic.net/content/

Complete Vocal Technique (CVT)
Research site
> http://cvtresearch.com/welcome/

Institute for Vocal Advancement (IVA)

"IVA is an organization that offers singers a method of vocal technique that is developed and refined as an outgrowth of our uncompromising search for truth and knowledge regarding the workings of the human voice."

https://www.vocaladvancement.com/about-iva/

International Association for Voice Movement Therapy

"An organization of practitioners which promotes the work of Voice Movement Therapy; maintains its core principles and standards; provides a forum for the exchange of ideas, information and experience; and reports on new developments, through conferences, publications, and other events."

http://www.iavmt.org

International Voice Teachers of Mix (IVTOM)

"IVTOM is a professional organization for voice teachers. We provide ongoing education, a mentor program, resources, international conferences, and a network for our members. IVTOM members include new voice teachers who are just beginning to develop the craft of teaching mix; highly trained professionals who hold degrees and certifications from the world's best universities and associations; and specialized experts, including otolaryngologists, speech pathologists, and voice scientists, who give us unparalleled access to medical and scientific information about the human voice."

http://www.ivtom.org

Johns Hopkins Peabody Conservatory

Online vocal pedagogy resources

http://peabody.jhu.edu/life-at-peabody/career-services/professional-resources/

Journal of the International Phonetic Association (JIPA)

"JIPA is especially concerned with the theory behind the International Phonetic Alphabet and publishes papers, known as Illustrations of the IPA, that use the alphabet for the analysis and description of the sound structures of a wide variety of languages."

https://www.cambridge.org/core/journals/journal-of-the- international-phonetic-association

Journal of Singing (JOS)
"Journal of Singing is the official journal of National Association of Teachers of Singing, providing current information regarding the teaching of singing as well as results of recent research in the field. A refereed journal, it serves as an historical record and is a venue for teachers of singing and other scholars to share the results of their work in areas such as history, diction, voice science, medicine, and especially voice pedagogy."

https://www.nats.org/cgi/page.cgi/about_journal_singing.html

(The) Modern Vocalist World
"Website accessing a monthly pay site dealing with Singing and Training Techniques, Singing Review and Feedback, Articles/Gear Reviews/Interviews, Singing Programs and Teachers, Vocal Gear, Seeking vocalist/Vocalist Available."

www.themodernvocalistworld.com

Musical America
The bible of all musical resources! Contact lists for all national and international music festivals, schools, auditions, agents, opera companies, contests, artists, managers, choral groups, plus much more.

https://www.musicalamerica.com/

National Association of Teachers of Singing (NATS)
"The largest professional association of teachers of singing in the world. Mission Statement: To encourage the highest standards of the vocal art and of ethical principles in the teaching of singing; and to promote vocal education and research at all levels, both for the enrichment of the general public and for the professional advancement of the talented."

https://www.nats.org

National Opera Association (NOA)
"The NOA seeks to promote a greater appreciation of opera and music theatre, to enhance pedagogy and performing activities, and to increase performance opportunities by supporting projects that improve the scope and quality of opera."

http://www.noa.org

National Center for Voice and Speech (NCVS)

"The NCVS conducts research, educates vocologists, disseminates information about voice and speech, and provides referral services in order to help people around the world enjoy healthy and effective vocal communications."

http://www.ncvs.org/about_mission.html

New York Singing Teachers' Association (NYTSA)

"NYSTA strives to provide voice professionals, both locally and globally, with the tools and inspiration needed for an increasingly informed and creative pedagogy. Immense advances in voice science, neurology, psychology, education theory, medicine, and mind/body healing offer new information and techniques from which voice teachers can draw. By making these resources accessible to our members, we foster twenty-first-century pedagogy, rooted in the great traditions of the past, incorporating the new knowledge of our time."

http://www.nyst.org/content/about-nysta

Opera America

"Opera America draws on resources and expertise from within and beyond the opera field to advance a mutually beneficial agenda that serves and strengthens the field (of opera)."

https://www.operaamerica.org

Opera Companies—List of Major Houses

At-a-glance list and URLs of the professional, semiprofessional, academic, and amateur companies and festivals offering regular programs of opera around the world.

http://opera.stanford.edu/companies.html

Singwise

Blogs, vocal topics, resources, and workshops for singers.

http://www.singwise.com/

Vocalist

"A resource for singers and singing teachers where you can find free online singing lessons, learn to sing with articles on voice/auditions/performing or working in the music industry. Includes articles for singing teachers and students of voice of all ages, standards and styles."

http://www.vocalist.org.uk/index.html

Vocal Pedagogy Research Guide: Home/Books
"This guide focuses on resources specifically meant for the private voice teacher, rather than the singer. . . . The resources listed are aimed for the more advanced researcher and musician but are also accessible to the beginner. Classical, popular, and musical theater pedagogy and voice science resources are included. . . ."

http://libguides.lib.umt.edu/vocalpedagogy

Vocapedia.info
"Educational resources relevant to the anatomic and physiologic basic of singing, the acoustics of the singing voice; the acoustical basis of resonance the physical health of the vocal mechanism the science of learning and mental processes involved in singing and teaching of singing current and historical thought on pedagogical practice." National Association of Teachers of Singing (NATS).

http://www.vocapedia.info/

Voice Council magazine
Vocal health, technique, gear, reviews, videos, mobile music, getting gigs, artists, bloggers.

http://www.voicecouncil.com

Vocology Quick Reference Guide
https://docs.google.com/document/d/1vabw5q-8j4ynCeNuYx24G6L5TQzEWnqtKD-dfmXyDyn8/edit#heading=herirg6scnij

VOCAL HEALTH

American Laryngological Association (ALA)
"Founded in 1878, the ALA is a scholarly organization of physicians and scientists who have made significant contributions to the care of patients with disorders of the larynx and upper aerodigestive tract."

https://alahns.org

American Speech-Language Hearing Association (ASHA)
"ASHA is the national professional, scientific, and credentialing association for 191,500 members and affiliates who are audiologists; speech-language pathologists; speech, language, and hearing scientists; audiology and speech-language pathology support personnel. Speech-language pathologists identify, assess, and treat speech and language problems, including swallowing disorders."

http://www.asha.org/about/

British Voice Association (BVA)
"The BVA is the 'voice for voice' in the UK, an association of multi-disciplinary professionals who work to promote the field of voice in its broadest sense."

http://www.britishvoiceassociation.org.uk/about.htm

Florida Center for Professional Voice

http://www.singershealth.com/

International Association of Phonosurgery
Phonosurgery includes surgical procedures that maintain, restore, or enhance the human voice.

http://www.md.ucl.ac.be/iap/

Johns Hopkins Voice Center
Speech and Voice Disorders

https://www.hopkinsmedicine.org/otolaryngology/specialty_areas/laryngology/voice/

Journal of the Acoustical Society of America (JASA)
"JASA has been the leading source of theoretical and experimental research results in the broad interdisciplinary subject of sound. The journal serves physical scientists, life scientists, engineers, psychologists, physiologists, architects, musicians, and speech communication specialists."

http://asa.scitation.org/jas/info/about

Journal of Speech, Language, and Hearing Research (JSLHR)
"JSLHR publishes peer-reviewed research and other scholarly articles on the normal and disordered processes in speech, language, hearing, and related areas such as cognition, oral-motor function, and swallowing."

http://jslhr.pubs.asha.org/ss/aboutJSLHR.aspx

(The) Journal of Voice

"[W]idely regarded as the world's premiere journal for voice medicine and research."

    http://www.jvoice.org/

Lion Voice Clinic

University of Minnesota

    http://www.lionsvoiceclinic.umn.edu/page7.htm#LARYNGECTOMY

National Center for Voice and Speech (NCVS)

"The NCVS conducts research, educates vocologists, disseminates information about voice and speech, and provides referral services in order to help people around the world enjoy healthy and effective vocal communications."

    http://www.ncvs.org/about_mission.html

Singershealth.com

National Institute for Continuing Education in Voice

Voice Foundation

"The world's oldest and leading organization dedicated to voice research, medicine, science, and education. The Voice Foundation is committed to enhancing the gift of vocal communication through research, education, publishing and raising awareness."

    http://voicefoundation.org

(The) Voice Workshop

"Provides cutting-edge vocal information for singers, singing teachers, colleges, universities, conservatories, corporations and those who work with or care for the voice. The information we provide is based upon the latest voice science and medicine as well as more than 45 years professional experience in the field of voice training and care, most particularly in professional singing in New York City."

    http://www.thevoiceworkshop.com

Wake Forest Baptist Medical Center

Voice and Swallowing Disorders & Treatment

    http://www.wakehealth.edu/Voice/

APPENDIX

TOOLS FOR THE SINGER

Appcompanist

Highly recommended by this author! "Control the world's best piano accompaniment recording with your smartphone. Any tempo, any key, any time."

https://www.appcompanist.com/

(The) Aria Database

"Besides providing basic information about each aria, the Database includes translations for many arias and aria texts for those that are not affected by copyright restrictions. The Database also provides access to a collection of operatic sound files to give visitors an idea of what each aria sounds like. It also contains information on available scores and sound files that can be purchased to aid in study and enjoyment."

http://www.aria-database.com/

(The) LiederNet Archive

"The world's largest reference archive of texts and translations of art songs & choral works."

http://www.lieder.net/lieder/index.html

Singer Savvy

"It allows you to check and log various aspects of your vocal usage and health throughout the day. You can assess your daily vocal function, how your voice is feeling, water intake, vocal naps, and set a vocal activity budget. While this app is not available in the App Store, once you set up a free account, you can follow the directions on the website to install an icon on your phone. There is also a lot of excellent vocal health advice on this app!"

www.singersavvyapp.com

Slatable

"Video Audition app. This app helps you to streamline the self-tape video audition process by providing easy title cards, editing tools, headshot uploads, even reader recordings for scenes. Video auditions are more and more common, and pre-screens are becoming the norm for college auditions, so it is nice to be able to create very professional-looking videos more easily."

https://www.slatable.com/

SmartMusic
"SmartMusic is a web-based music education platform that connects teachers and students. Teachers have access to an unrivaled library of music from which to create individualized assignments for every student. Students receive immediate feedback as they practice each assignment. Their best performances are sent back to the teacher for grading and additional guidance. Plus, built-in notation tools allow teachers to import, edit, and create music, producing custom content for their students."

https://www.smartmusic.com

Vocal Masterclassics
"Vocal Masterclassics is an easily searchable Institutional Database Resource that provides voice students and faculty with complete documentation, program information, and access to the world's great vocal masterclasses."

https://vocalmasterclassics.com

YAP Tracker
"Use this site to find and track up to 3000 opera auditions, Resident Artist Programs and vocal competitions a year."

https://www.yaptracker.com

MUSICAL THEATER RESOURCES

Backstage
Resource for all things Musical Theater.

https://www.backstage.com/

(The) College Audition Blog
Musical theatre, opera, music ed, acting, and more

https://auditioningforcollege.com/

Musical Theater Resources
"This blog was created to share a variety of musical theatre resources with performers and teachers, including theatre voice training information, repertoire lists, audition advice, interviews, and much more."

https://musicaltheatreresources.com/tag/vocal-pedagogy/

StageAgent
Leading resource for everything musical theater.
http://stageagent.com/

CONTEMPORARY COMMERCIAL MUSIC (CCM)

Complete Vocal Institute
Most recommended by this author for learning contemporary styles of singing in the most scientific way. "The CVI Vocal Academy teaches how to combine the four elements of the Complete Vocal Technique to students who can then design the voice they want to work with and produce precisely the sounds they want. They will also be able to pinpoint their specific problems and mistakes and focus on which techniques they wish to work on. The four main elements are: 1. The three overall principles—to ensure healthy sound production. 2. The four vocal modes—to choose the 'gear' you want to sing in. 3. Sound colors—to make the sound lighter or darker. 4. Effects—to achieve specific sound effects."
http://completevocal.institute

Estill Voice International
"Estill Voice Training encourages those who seek vocal versatility to explore the full range of expression in the human voice, but not at the expense of vocal well-being."
https://www.estillvoice.com

Hennessy Breath & Bodywork
"Whole body exercises for singers and actors."
https://www.hennessybb.com

Institute for Vocal Advancement (IVA)
"The foundation of what we teach is vocal balance. We believe that this is the key to ensuring success in a singer's voice. Vocal balance gives singers the ability to control their voices while singing any style of music. It allows them to sound free and natural. We think a singer should be able to access all dynamic levels in their voice without straining, cracking, or breaking."
https://www.vocaladvancement.com/en-us/about-iva

Speech Level Singing International: The SLS Method
Seth Riggs
http://www.speechlevelsinging.com/slsmethod.html

Voice Lessons to the World
New York Vocal Coaching Inc.
https://voicelessonstotheworld.com/

FACEBOOK SINGERS' GROUPS AND COMMUNITIES

Art Song Liedership Group for the 21st Century
https://www.facebook.com/groups/456320144943173/?hc_location=group

(The) Business of Singing Forum
https://www.facebook.com/groups/1756680741215336/

Born 2 Sing Kids
https://www.facebook.com/Born-2-Sing-Kids-586901061434699/

Colleagues in Singing and Performance
"A place for serious discussions about the idea of singing and performance."
https://www.facebook.com/groups/1420490751547081/

(The) Daily Listen: Great Singers, Great Singing
https://www.facebook.com/groups/173955173223216/

Estill Voice Training
https://www.facebook.com/estillvoice/

Find Your Singing Teacher
https://www.facebook.com/groups/findyoursingingteacher/about/

Functional Voice Book Club—LIVE!
https://www.facebook.com/groups/333221407108328/

Hal Leonard/Vocal
https://www.facebook.com/halleonardvocal/

Middle School Chorus Directors
https://www.facebook.com/groups/265422856991494/about/

Music Teachers
https://www.facebook.com/groups/musicpln

Music Teacher's Resources
https://www.facebook.com/MusicTeacherResources4U

Music Teacher's National Association
https://www.facebook.com/mtnapage

Musical Theatre Voice Teachers & Coaches Network
https://www.facebook.com/groups/musicaltheatrevoiceteachers/

(A) New Forum for Professional Voice Teachers
https://www.facebook.com/groups/1810591335659853/

(The) New Forum for Classical Singers Group (NFCS)
https://www.facebook.com/groups/NFCSGroup/

Opera America
https://www.facebook.com/operaamerica/

Opera Singer Memes
https://www.facebook.com/OperaSingerMemes/

Popular & Commercial Music Voice Teachers
https://www.facebook.com/groups/214393498953137

Professional Voice Teachers
https://www.facebook.com/groups/professionalvoiceteachers/

Singing Answers for Teachers and Students
https://www.facebook.com/groups/1515243511853170/about/

Singing Lessons for Little Singers
https://www.facebook.com/littlesingers/

Talk Classical
https://www.talkclassical.com/54418-problem-fach-system-5.html

Vocalogical Conversations
https://www.facebook.com/groups/VocalogicalConversations/members/

Vocology In Practice
https://www.facebook.com/vocologyinpractice/

Voice Geek Group
https://www.facebook.com/groups/VoiceGeek

Voice Instruction
https://www.facebook.com/voiceinstruction

Voice Teacher's Community
https://www.facebook.com/groups/voiceteacherscommunity/

Voice Teachers for Young Singers
https://www.facebook.com/groups/VoiceTeachers
forYoungSingers/

Voice Training
https://www.facebook.com/voicetrainnnig

Voice Training for Nonclassical Singing
https://www.facebook.com/groups/6553882477

IPHONE AND IPAD APPS

Aria Search
https://itunes.apple.com/us/app/aria-search/id1254706977?mt=8

Art Song
https://itunes.apple.com/us/app/art-song/id1251442936?mt=8

French Diction for Singers
https://itunes.apple.com/us/app/fre-diction/id697814621?mt=8

German Diction for Singers
https://itunes.apple.com/us/app/ger-diction/id683642668?mt=8

IPA for Singers
https://itunes.apple.com/us/app/ipa-sing/id670630052?mt=8

Italian Diction for Singers
https://itunes.apple.com/us/app/it-diction/id673429524?mt=8

Musical Theater Songs
https://itunes.apple.com/us/app/it-diction/id673429524?mt=8

Repertoire Apps—Bundle

"This bundle contains Art Song, Musical Theatre Songs and Aria Search. These three apps include over 10,000 searchable songs and arias from the standard repertoire. Within each app, you can listen to YouTube clips of songs/arias and create a favorites playlist."

https://itunes.apple.com/us/app-bundle/repertoire-apps/id1266402558?mt=8

Vocalizer—Singing

https://play.google.com/store/apps/details?id=com.hectorricardo.vocprim

BIBLIOGRAPHY

BOOKS

American Psychiatric Association (2013). *Diagnostic and Statistical Manual of Mental Disorders*. 5th ed. DSM-5: Washington, DC: American Psychiatric Publishing.

Clark, M. (2002). *Singing, Acting, and Movement in Opera: A Guide to Singer-getics*. Bloomington: Indiana University Press.

Coffin, B. (1980). *Overtones of Bel Canto*. Metuchen, NJ: Scarecrow Press.

Coffin, Errolle, Singer, DeLattre (1994). *Phonetic Readings of Songs and Arias*. 2nd ed. New Jersey: Scarecrow Press.

Crelin, E. (1987). *The Human Vocal Tract: Anatomy, Function, Development, and Evolution*. New York: Vantage Press.

Doscher, B. (1994). *The Functional Unity of the Singing Voice*. Metuchen, NJ: Scarecrow Press.

Dunning, D. (2005). *Self-insight: Roadblocks and Detours on the Path to Knowing Thyself*. London: Psychology Press.

Emmons, S., and Sonntag, S. (1979). *The Art of the Song Recital*. New York: Schirmer.

Fields, V. A. (1950). *Training the Singing Voice: An Analysis of the Working Concepts Contained in Recent Contributions to Vocal Pedagogy*. New York: King's Crown Press.

Kagen, S. (1950). *On Studying Singing*. New York: Dove Publications.

Marafioti, P. M. (1933). *Caruso's Method of Voice Production: The Scientific Culture of the Voice*. New York: D. Appleton.

Malde, M., Allen, M., Zeller, K. (2009). *What Every Singer Needs to Know About the Body*. San Diego: Plural Publishing.

Maurice, G. (2013). *Finding Vocal Artistry.* Maurice: Xlibris.
McKinney, J. (2005). *The Diagnosis and Correction of Vocal Faults.* Rev. ed. Nashville, TN: Genevox Music Group.
Miller, D. (2008). *Resonance in Singing: Voice Building through Acoustic Feedback.* Princeton: Inside View Press.
Miller, R. (1986). *The Structure of Singing: A System and Art in Vocal Technique.* New York: Schirmer Books.
Miller, R. (1996). *On the Art of Singing.* Oxford, England: Oxford University Press.
Nair, G. (1999). *Voice Tradition and Technology: A State-of-the-art Studio.* San Diego: Singular Press Group.
Reid, C. (1950). *Bel Canto: Principles and Practices.* New York: Coleman-Ross.
Reid, C. (1975). *Psyche and Soma.* New York: Patelson Music House.
Reid, C. (1983). *A Dictionary of Vocal Terminology: An Analysis.* New York: Patelson Music House.
Sacks, P. (1999). *Generation X Goes to College: An Eye-opening Account of Teaching in Postmodern America.* Chicago: Open Court.
Sills, B. (1987). *Beverly: An Autobiography.* New York: Bantam Books.
Smith, B., and Sataloff, R. (2006). *Choral Pedagogy.* 2nd ed. San Diego: Plural Publishing.
Smith, W. S. (2007). *The Naked Voice: A Wholistic Approach to Singing.* New York, Oxford University Press.
Sundberg, J. (1987). *The Science of the Singing Voice.* DeKalb: Northern Illinois University Press.
Twenge, J. (2009). *The Narcissism Epidemic: Living in the Age of Entitlement.* New York: Simon & Schuster.
Wall, J. (1989). *International Phonetic Alphabet for Singers: A Manual for English and Foreign Language Diction.* Greenbank, WA: Pacific Isle Publishing.
Ware, C. (1998). *Basics of Vocal Pedagogy: The Foundations and Process of Singing.* Boston: McGraw-Hill.

OTHER SOURCES

Bloothooft, G., and Plomp, R. (1986). "The Sound Level of the Singer's Formant in Professional Singing." *Journal of the Acoustical Society of America*, 79, 2028–2033, https://pubmed.ncbi.nlm.nih.gov/3722610/

Breslow, G. D. (2017). "The Voice Lift: How and Why Vocal Rejuvenation Surgery is Performed." *Zwivel: Fillers Guide.* https://www.zwivel.com/blog/what-is-voice-lift-surgery/.

Chicago Tribune (2018). "The Health Benefits of Singing a Tune." *Chicago Tribune.* https://www.chicagotribune.com/suburbs/advertising/todayshealthywoman/ct-ss-thw-health-benefits-of-singing-a-tune-20180314dto-story.html

Cleveland Clinic (2020). "Leukoplakia." *Cleveland Clinic.* https://my.clevelandclinic.org/health/diseases/17655-leukoplakia.

Dhillon, V. K. (2020). "What Are the Symptoms of Vocal Cord Disorders?" *Johns Hopkins Medicine.* https://www.hopkinsmedicine.org/health/conditions-and-diseases/vocal-cord-disorders.

Dunning, D. (2005). "Essays in Social Psychology. Self-insight: Roadblocks and Detours on the Path to Knowing Thyself." *Psychology Press.* https://scirp.org/reference/ReferencesPapers.aspx?ReferenceID=1416557.

Dunning, D., and Kruger, J. (1999). "Unskilled and Unaware of It: How Difficulties in Recognizing One's Own Incompetence Lead to Inflated Self-Assessments." *Journal of Personality and Social Psychology* 77(6), 1121–1134.

Emmons, S. (2010). "UPDATE! On Breath Management." *Focus on Vocal Technique.* www.sci.brooklyn.cuny.edu/~jones/Shirlee/Underwood.html.

Emmons, S. (2010). "The Tongue as Master of Your Singing: Vowel Modification." *Focus on Vocal Technique.* http://www.sci.brooklyn.cuny.edu/~jones/Shirlee/tongue.html.

Felman, A. (2019). "What to Know about Antibiotics." *Medical News Today Newsletter.* https://www.medicalnewstoday.com/articles/10278.

Fields, V. A. (1972). "How Mind Governs Voice." *NATS* Bulletin 22, no. 2: 2-10.

Frosh, A., and Elkins L. (2012). "From Eating Too Much to Antibiotics: What's Caused the Frog in YOUR Throat?" *Daily Mail Health.* www.dailymail.co.uk/health/article-2224983/From-eating-antibiotics-Whats-caused-frog-YOUR-throat.html.

Gabbey, A., and Gotter, A. (2019). "Deviated Septum." *Healthline.* https://www.healthline.com/health/deviated-septum.

Giobbi, M. (2020). "Mindfulness Through Music: An Introduction." *Psychology Today.* https://www.psychologytoday.com/us/blog/mindfulness-and-music/202003/mindfulness-through-music-introduction.

Gordan, E. (2020). "Audiation." *Gordon Institute for Music Learning.* https://giml.org/mlt/audiation/.

Gregg, J. W. (1991). "From Song to Speech: On Articulation–Part II." *NATS Journal* 47, 1: 25, 39.

Gupta, R. (2019). "Singers and Steroids: 'The Magic Pill.'" *Osborne Head & Neck Institute.* https://www.ohniww.org/singers-and-steroids-voice-effects/.

Ingmire, J. (2015). "Acquiring 'Perfect Pitch' May Be Possible for Adults." *UChicago News.* https://news.uchicago.edu/story/acquiring-perfect-pitch-may-be-possible-some-adults#:~:text=Acquiring.

InnerDrive. (2020). "What to Think About Before a Match." *InnerDrive*: Blog. https://blog.innerdrive.co.uk/sports/what-to-think-about-before-a-match.

Kingston, H. (2019). "Hypothyroidism Symptoms Checklist: Hot to Spot an Under-active Thyroid." *Let's Get Checked.* https://www.letsgetchecked.com/articles/hypothyroidism-symptoms-checklist-underactive-thyroid/?imp=cpc&lgc_code=SELFCARE&lgc_saving=30&gclid=Cj0KCQjws536BR DTARIsANeUZ5-TV7B8erAbL0JMKzaTZxUs9s6YTAsQA6v LWQ_QgjuYIc7CGBY8s5YaAifnEALw_wcB.

Kirkwood, C. (March 24, 2015). "Myelin: An Overview." *Brainfacts.org: Research & Discoveries*. https://www.brainfacts.org/brain-anatomy-and-function/anatomy/2015/myelin.

Marks, L. (2015). "What Is an Analgesic?" *Everyday Health*. https://www.everydayhealth.com/analgesic/guide/.

Mayo Clinic, (2020). "Laryngology and Voice Disorders: Overview." *Mayo Clinic*. https://www.mayoclinic.org/departments-centers/laryngology-and-voice-disorders/overview/ovc-20426888.

McGlashan, J. (2016). "Understanding Laryngeal Stroboscopy." *CVT Research*. https://cvtresearch.com/understanding-laryngeal-stroboscopy/.

McIntosh, J. (2019). "Symptoms and Treatment of Bronchitis." *Medical News Today*. https://www.medicalnewstoday.com/articles/8888.

Merck Manual, (2020). "Laryngeal Contact Ulcers—Ear, Nose, and Throat Disorders." *Merck Manual*. https://www.merckmanuals.com/professional/ear-nose-and-throat-disorders/laryngeal-disorders/laryngeal-contact-ulcers.

Medical Centric, (2018). "Boggart-Bacall Syndrome (BBS), *Medical Centric*, youtube.com/watch?v=tXNV_FP5e3o.

Michael, D. (2020). "Irritable Larynx Syndrome (ILS)." *LionsVOICEclinic*. http://www.lionsvoiceclinic.umn.edu/page5.htm#PVFM.

Morrison, T. (2017). "What Is a Frenulectomy or Frenectomy? (Reasons and Indications)." *Houston Ear, Nose, Throat, and Allergy*. https://www.houstonent.com/blog/what-is-a-frenulectomy-reasons-and-indications-children-adults.

Murphy, A. (2020). "AAAAI Allergy and Asthma Drug Guide." *AAAAI Ask the Expert*. https://www.aaaai.org/conditions-and-treatments/drug-guide.

NIH (2020). "Spasmadic Dysphonia." *NIDCD*. https://www.nidcd.nih.gov/health/spasmodic-dysphonia.

O'Conner, K. (2020). "Singing While Pregnant." *Singwise*. https://www.singwise.com/articles/singing-while-pregnant.

Pantono, K. (2015). "History of the Laryngoscope." *ENTtoday*. www.enttoday.org/article/history-of-the-laryngoscope/.

Pietrangelo, A., and Nall, R. (2019). "Everything You Want to Know About Tonsillitis." *Healthline*. https://www.healthline.com/health/tonsillitis.

Ragen, K., and Gangopadhyay, K. (2012). "Intubation Considerations for Singers." *Journal of Singing* 69, no. 1: 43–46.

Sasaki, C. (2020). "Laryngeal Contact Ulcers." *Merck Manual*. https://www.merckmanuals.com/professional/ear,-nose,-and-throat-disorders/laryngeal-disorders/laryngeal-contact-ulcers.

Sheils, P. (2020). "TMJ and Rejuvenation Dentistry." *Otsego Dental*. https://otsegodental.com/tmj-rejuvenation-dentistry/.

Sundberg, J. (1977). "The Acoustics of the Singing Voice." *Scientific American* 236, 3: 82–91. http://www.music.mcgill.ca/~gary/courses/papers/Sundberg_SingingVoice_ScientificAmerican_1977.pdf.

Sutton, L. (2017). "How Does Sleep Affect My Voice?" *Charlotte Eye Ear Nose & Throat Assoc.*, P.A. https://www.ceenta.com/news-blog/how-does-sleep-affect-my-voice#:~:text=If%20you%20sing%20while%20your,most%20common%20cause%20of%20hoarseness.

Swanson, L. (2018). "Singing Through Menopause." *ChoralNet*. https://choralnet.org/2018/07/singing-through-menopause/#:~:text=Estrogen%20deprivation%20causes%20substantial%20changes,to%20increase%20(Emerich%2C%20Hoover.

Watterson, T. (2020). "The Use of the Nasometer and Interpretation of Nasalance Scores." *Ashawire*. https://pubs.asha.org/doi/10.1044/2019_PERSP-19-00029.

Web MD (2019). "Adenoiditis." *WebMD*. https://www.webmd.com/children/adenoiditis#1-3.

Web MD (2019). "Do I Need Antihistamines for Allergies?" *WebMD*. https://www.webmd.com/allergies/antihistamines-for-allergies.

Whitten, S. (2006). "Acid Reflux." *Boston Singer's Resource*. https://www.bostonsingersresource.org/resources/vocal-health/vocal-health-articles/acid-reflux#:~:text=As%20singers%20our%20lifestyles%20and,job%20or%20job%20to%20rehearsals.

INDEX

Note: Page numbers in *italics* indicate exercises.

Academy of Teachers of Singing (AATS), 170–174, 213
acoustic cage, 57, 59
Alexander Technique, 148
alignment. *See* posture/alignment
anatomy of human voice, formants and, 41–42
anosognosia, 30
Appelman, D. Ralph, 43
appoggio, definition and explanation, 95–96
appoggio exercises, 96–99, 163–164
   Beach Ball, *98–99*
   Ice Skating, *163*
   Icing the Cake, *163*
   The Motorcycle Throttle, *163*
   Pointing Down While Going Up, *163–164*
   Straw Technique, *97–98*
   Sucking Through the Hand and Tending to the Arm, *96–97*
   Walking the Table, *109–110, 164*
   The Wall Push, *99*
artistry, 20–21
aspirate onset, 85
aspirate release, 88
assessment lesson, 174–175

awareness of singing abilities. *See* self-perception

Back to front text prep, 135–137
balanced release, 88
Balancing the Breath (inhale/exhale/phonate/sustain tone), *90–93*
baritone, 178, 181, 183–184, 185
bass, 178, 181, 182, 183–184, 185
bass-baritone, 178, 183–184, 185
Beach Ball, *98–99*
bel canto (beautiful singing). *See also* imagination
   artistry and, 20–21
   CCM vocal technique and, 103–104
   defined, 7
   desire and, 21
   imitation and (*See* imitation)
   mental imagery and, 23–24
   positive feedback and, 22, 33
   technique, 7–8
   this book and, 9–10
   unity and, 19–20
Bell, Alexander Graham, 42
belly laughing. *See* Skipping the Rock/Belly Laughing

INDEX

Bend to the Floor, *166*
Bernoulli Principle, 83–84
beta blockers, 196
Big Fog vs. Small Fog, *83*
blocking, memorizing and, 138, 142, 145
body, singing and. *See also* hand movements *references*; hearing; posture/alignment
  about: overview of, 147
  anatomy of human voice, 41–42
  forehead tension, 152
  imitation value and, 25, 160–161
  lip tension, 152–153
  natural effects on the voice, 153–155
  smiling's effect on singing, 153
  warming up (*See* warm-ups, body)
Boyajian, Armen, 13
breath and breathing
  about: overview/summary of, 77–78, 110
  CCM vocal technique *bel canto* relationship, 103–104
  connecting the cords, 99–103
  correct intake and release, 79–80
  engaging pure vowels, 80
  exercises (*See* breathing exercises)
  falling into the breath, 89–90
  focus, placement and, 89
  inflections, glides and, 105–107
  Lamperti on, 59, 66, 77, 78, 82, 84, 87, 89, 90, 95, 99
  management and connection, 78–80
  messa de voce and, 105
  nose vs. mouth inhalation, 81
  by note length (whole, dotted half, half, quarter notes), 81–82
  onset of tone (glottal/aspirate/coordinated) and, 84–85
  phonation and, 83–85
  playing the voice, 87
  quick breath before onset, 85–87
  release of tone (aspirate/glottal/balanced/flaring) and, 87–88
  resonance and, 60 (*See also* resonance)
  rhythmic breathing, 81–82
  stage fright and, 197
  supporting the breath, 95
  throat position during inhalation, 82–83
  tone onset and, 84–87
breathing exercises. *See also appoggio* exercises
  about: for clearing airy tone/connecting the cords, 100–103; for forward movement, 109–110; for quick breath before onset, 85–87; for throat position during inhalation, 82–83
  Balancing the Breath (inhale/exhale/phonate/sustain tone), 90–93
  Big Fog vs. Small Fog, *83*
  The Creaking Door, *100–101*
  The Cry/welp, *86*
  The Crystal Glass, *108–109*
  Exciting the Breath: Fogging the Mirror, *93–94*
  Frisbee, *92*
  Glide and Inflection, *107–108*
  Jaw and Breath, *83*
  The Lasso, *108*
  The Long Tone, *86*
  The Monkey/The Insect, *101–103*
  Open Feeling, *85–86*

INDEX

Skipping the Rock/Belly Laughing, *93*
Spiking the Volleyball, *86–87*
Tennis (Backhand Swing), *92–93*
Using the Stage Voice, *100*
Walking the Table, *109–110, 164*
Brown, William E., 10
"building on the soft," 66

C**CM**, 103–104, 222–223
chiaroscuro (chiaro and oscuro), 40, 46, 48, 53, 76, 102
choral habits, correcting poor, 194–195
closing consonants, 122
Coffin, Berton, 45, 58
competence
    conscious competence, 33
    conscious incompetence, 33
    narcissism and, 30–32
    self-perception and, 29–32
    stages of, 32–33
    unconscious competence, 33
    unconscious incompetence, 33
conception, 28–29
confidence
    competence and, 32–33
    getting the head out of the way, 27
    narcissism and, 30–32
    overcoming obstacles for (*See* vocal problems, addressing)
    playing the voice and, 87
    preparedness and (*See* song preparation)
    sense of lack/limitation and, 18–19
    stage fright and, 19, 26, 195–197
    teachers building, 154–155

visualization and, 26
vocal image and, 24, 35–36
connecting
    the cords, 99–103
    to core sound in recitative, 137–138
    management and connection, 78–80
    syllables, 129–130
    voice to text, 111–112
conscious competence, 33
conscious incompetence, 33
conservatory, training at, 116–117, 214
consonants, 122–127. *See also* language; song preparation; vowels
    about: overview/formation of, 122–123
    categories of, 122
    closing, 122
    constricting, 122
    diverting, 122
    double, in Italian, *127*
    exercises, *124, 126–127*
    International Phonetic Alphabet (IPA), 118–120
    K, T, and P endings, 128–129
    leaping to higher pitch, *125–126*
    low vs. high, 123
    unwritten double, 123–125
    using before large leaps, *126–127*
constricting consonants, 122
Contemporary Commercial Music (CCM), 103–104, 222–223
contralto, 177, 178, 184. *See also* vocal registers and range
coordinated onset, 85
coordination of voice aspects, 54–55
countertenor, 178–179, 185
covering, 69–70

The Creaking Door, *100–101*
The Cry/welp, *86*
The Crystal Glass, *108–109*

DeLattre, Pierre, 45, 120
desire, as first step in singing, 21
desire, motivation and, 21–22. *See also* motivation
diction, 120
diphthongs, 129
diverting consonants, 122
Doscher, Barbara, 43
Dunning, David, 29
Dunning-Kruger effect, 29, 30

Ears. *See* hearing
education. *See also* voice teachers and students
    finding right voice teacher (*See* voice teachers and students)
    learning and singing in foreign language, 115–118
    music (well-rounded) importance, 169
Emmons, Shirlee, 58, 96–97, 142
enunciation. *See* language; text
environment, effect on voice, 154
Exciting the Breath: Fogging the Mirror, *93–94*
exercises. *See also appoggio* exercises; breathing exercises; resonance exercises
    for consonants, *124, 126–127*
    for visualization, *26*
    for vowels, *121–122*
expectations, narcissism and, 31–32
extraneous vocal sounds, 130–131

Facebook groups/communities, 223–225
Fach system, 182–185
false vocal cords, 52–53
falsetto
    about, 178–179
    CCM vocal technique and, 103
    finding correct vocal tract placement, 66
    vocal range/registers and, 175, 176, 178–180, 182
feedback, positive, 22, 33
feeling, listening/hearing vs., 36–37, 155–157. *See also* mind connection
Feldenkreis Method, 148
Felix, Antonia, 13, 14
Felix, Stanford
    background and vocal journey, 10–15
    early experience leading to stage fright, 18–19
    high school and higher education, 12–13
    inspiration to sing, 11
    life-changing accident, 12–13
    teaching career, 13–14, 18
Finger above the Adam's Apple, *74–75*
flaring release, 88
floor, singing to, 149–150
focus, mental, 27–28
focus, placement and, 89
fog. *See* Big Fog vs. Small Fog; Exciting the Breath: Fogging the Mirror
forehead tension, 152
foreign language, learning and singing in, 115–118
formants
    anatomy of human voice and, 41–42
    avoiding damping of sound, 46–47, 48, 49

clustered (closed vowels), 43
definition and mechanics of,
    41–44
optimizing resonance and,
    46–49
separated (open vowels), 43
singer's, 44–49
software to detect, 45
tuning, 44–45
types of, 42–43
vowels and, 42–44, 120–121
Frisbee, 92

Garofalo, Marcello, 123–124
Giobbi, Matthew, 34
glides, *98, 99,* 105–*109, 163,* 181.
    See also inflections
glottal onset, 84–85
glottal release, 88
golden rule of singing, 23
golden rule of singing in time, 132

Hand movements during practice,
    161–164
    Ice Skating, *163*
    Icing the Cake, *163*
    The Motorcycle Throttle, *163*
    Pointing Down While Going
        Up, *163–164*
    Shoot the Pistol, *162*
    Throw the Dart, *162–163*
    Walking the Table, *164*
hand movements while
    performing, 164–165
Head Rolls, *165–166*
head, singing and. *See also* hearing;
    jaw
    about: things to monitor in
        mirror, 152–153
    forehead tension, 152
    lip tension, 152–153

natural effects on the voice,
    153–155
smiling's effect on singing, 153
health, vocal. *See* vocal health; vocal
    problems, addressing
hearing
    feeling vs., 36–37, 155, 156–157
    imitation, "good ear" and, 25
    listening vs., 155–156
    pitch and, 158–159
    before singing, 157
high consonants, 123

Ice Skating, *163*
Icing the Cake, *163*
illness, disorders. *See also* vocal
    disorders and faults
illness, practicing and, 189–190. *See
    also* vocal health; vocal problems,
    addressing
illusory superiority, 29. *See also* self-
    perception
imagery scale, 65
imagination
    exercise, *26*
    importance of, 26
    influencing outcomes, 26
    Lamperti on, 25, 149, 157
    mental imagery and, 23–24
    visualization and, 26, 127, 130,
        139
imitation
    of all types of sounds, 160–162
    importance/value of, 25, 160–161
    Ruffo learning to sing and, 160
    of voice personalities, 64–65
infections and glides, 105–107
inflections, 64–65, 105, *107–109,*
    161. *See also* glides
inhalation. *See* breath and
    breathing; breathing exercises

The Insect. *See* The Monkey/The Insect
International Phonetic Alphabet (IPA), 118–120
iPhone/iPad apps, 226–227
Italian, double consonants in, 127
Italian, learning and singing in, 115–118

Jaw
  Gross Chewing, *167*
  Jaw and Breath, *83*
  position, 61, *83*
  Relaxing the Jaw and Tongue, *166*
  resonance and, 61–62
  Rubbing Out the Jaw, *167*
  tension, 62
  warm-ups, 166–167
Jones, James Earl, 64

K, words ending with, 128–129
Kruger, Justin, 29. *See also* Dunning-Kruger effect

Lake Wobegon Effect, 30
Lamperti, Giovanni, on singing and
  about: this book and, 1–2, 10
  the act of singing, 29, 33
  anatomy/physiology, 95, 143, 147, 151
  attack being too hard, 84
  balancing intelligence and emotion, 35, 149
  breathing/diaphragm, 59, 66, 77, 78, 82, 84, 87, 89, 90, 95, 99
  broadening knowledge of literature, 20
  controlling your voice, 54
  difficulties in singing, 77, 198
  effort and energy, 90
  feeling, not listening to yourself, 155
  focused vowels, 71
  gaining control of our activities, 21
  hearing sense, 24, 157
  heart/mind and self-knowledge, 27
  imagination, 25, 149, 157
  knowing result before acting ('golden rule'), 23
  "knowing thyself," 17
  and language/words/phrases, 111, 112, 113, 114
  maintaining unity, 19
  natualness of singing, 7
  practicing/exercises, 185, 188
  resonance, 39, 44, 46, 54, 57, 66, 71
  subjective readiness to sing, 139
  tone, 50, 51, 78, 84, 151
  tone emerging from silence, 87
  tone vs. noise, 41
  tone's focus, 89
  vibration, 49, 51, 54, 56, 71, 99, 114
  when you can sing, 28
Langan, Kevin, 1–2
language. *See also* consonants; song preparation; text; vowels
  connecting syllables, 129–130
  diction, 120
  diphthongs, 129
  extraneous vocal sounds, 130–131
  foreign, learning and singing in, 115–118
  International Phonetic Alphabet (IPA), 118–120
  K, T, and P endings, 128–129

INDEX

memorization, 143–145
projection, 114–115
speech vs. singing, 113
understanding, "singer mode" and, 112–113
laryngeal collar, 51–52
larynx
   acoustic cage and, 57
   engaging lips and lowering, 57–58, 80
   exercises for lowering, 72–76
   jaw tension and lowering, 62
   laryngeal collar and lowering, 51–52
   lowered, raised soft palate and, 40, 62–63, 64, 72–76
   quick breath before onset and, 86
   resonance and, 46, 62–63, 72–76
   throat position during inhalation, 82–83
The Lasso, *108*
lips
   crossover between genres and, 67–69
   engaging for resonance, 57–59
   smiling's effect on singing, 153
   tension in, 152–153
   vowel placement and, 70–71
   (*See also* vowels)
listening, hearing/feeling vs., 155–157
The Long Tone, *86*
A Loose Lowered Jaw #1, *73*
A Loose Lowered Jaw #2, *73*
low consonants, 123
Low Vowels, *74*

Marking and *sotto voce*, 66–67
mask, facial, 36–37, 56, 89, 101
McKinney, James, 51, 52
mechanistic teaching, 37, 38
memorizing, 143–145
   about: overview of, 143
   blocking and, 138, 142, 145
   rhythmically, 144–145
   visually, 143–144
messa de voce, 105
mezzo-soprano, 55, 177, 178, 181, 184. *See also* vocal registers and range
Miller, Donald Gray, 45
mind connection. *See also* confidence; imagination; imitation; motivation
   artistry and, 20–21
   attitude and intent, 34–35
   balancing intelligence and emotion, 35, 149
   conception, 28–29
   desire and, 21
   getting the head out of the way, 27
   importance of, 154–155
   Lamperti on heart-head uniting, 27
   mental focus, 27–28
   mental imagery, 23–24
   mind rather than voice that sings, 24
   mindfulness and, 34
   personality and, 35–36
   pitch and, 158–159
   self-perception and, 28, 29–32
   sense of lack/limitation and, 18–19
   unity and, 19–20
mindfulness, 34
modal voice, 176–177
Modified Vowels, *122*
The Monkey/The Insect, *101–103*
motivation

core, for singing, 23
desire and, 21–22
love of music and, 23
past experiences influencing,
    18–19
perspectives on singing and,
    21–23
positive feedback feeding, 22, 33
The Motorcycle Throttle, *163*
musical theater resources, 221–222

Nair, Garyth, 41
narcissism, 30–32
nasality, nose resonance vs., 55–56
nose
    inhalation, mouth inhalation
        vs., 81
    resonance vs. nasality, 55–56

On the Edge, 75–76
onset of tone
    aspirate onset, 85
    coordinated onset, 85
    glottal onset, 84–85
    quick breath before, 85–87
    types of, 84–85
Open Feeling, 85–86

P, words ending with, 128–129
Paper Towel Tube, 74
passaggio
    about, 180–181
    CCM vocal technique, *bel canto*
        and, 103
    covering and, 69–70
    falsetto and, 178
    main problem areas by voice,
        181
    mixing registers and, 182
    modal voice and, 176–177
    vocal registers and, 176

pedagogy. *See* voice teachers and
    students
pelvic tilt, 151
perfect pitch, 158–159
personality, 35–36
phonation
    about, 83–85
    Balancing the Breath (inhale/
        exhale/phonate/sustain tone),
        90–93
    equalizing breath before, 90
    exhaling for, 86
    onset of tone (glottal/aspirate/
        coordinated) and, 84–85
    throat position during
        inhalation and, 82–83
Pillars of the Throat, *75*
pitch, 158–159
Pointing Down While Going Up,
    163–164
poor pitch, 159
positive imagery visualization, 26
posture/alignment
    alignment methods, 148–149
    emotional alignment and, 149–150
    exercise, *74*
    importance of, 74
    muscle memory and habit
        formation, 151–152
    "Noble Position" described,
        147–148
    pelvic tilt and, 151
    poor, external causes, 150–151
    singing to the floor fix, 149–150
    stance, 150
practicing, 185–190
    amount/length of practice,
        188–189
    cool down, 188
    feeling the sound/vibration,
        36–37, 156–157

how practice works, 185–186
illness and, 189–190 (*See also* vocal health; vocal problems, addressing)
repertoire work, 187–188
setting the scene for, 186–187
steps to effective practice, 186–188
warm-up, 187 (*See also* warm-ups, body)
preparing songs. *See* song preparation
present, being in the moment, 34
problems. *See* vocal problems, addressing
projection
    mental imagery and, 24
    singing vs. speech, 114–115

Quasthof, Thomas, 17–18

Racik, Donna, 136
range. *See* vocal registers and range
registers. *See* vocal registers and range
Reid, C., 53, 105, 158
relative pitch, 159
relaxation techniques, 196
Relaxing the Jaw and Tongue, *166*
repertoire, work on, 187–188
resonance. *See also* formants
    about: overview/summary of, 39–40, 76
    acoustic cage and, 57, 59
    "building on the soft" and, 66
    coordination and, 54–55
    covering and, 69–70
    crossover between genres and, 67–69
    engaging lips for, 57–59
    false vocal cords and, 52–53
    formation of, 39–40
    imagery scale for stuck sound determination, 65
    inhalation and (*See* breath and breathing)
    jaw position and, 61
    jaw tension and, 62
    Lamperti on, 39, 44, 46, 54, 57, 66, 71
    laryngeal collar and, 51–52
    light-dark (*chiaroscuro*) and, 46, 48, 53, 76, 102
    marking, *sotto voce* and, 66–67
    nose resonance vs. nasality, 55–56
    raised soft palate/lowered larynx for, 62–63
    tessitura and, 55
    timbre and, 53–54
    tongue position and, 60–61
    tongue tension and, 61
    vibrato affecting, 50
    voice personalities and, 64–65
    volume and, 51
    vowel placement and, 70–71
    weight in the voice and, 71–72
resonance exercises
    about: overview of, 72–73
    Finger above the Adam's Apple, *74–75*
    A Loose Lowered Jaw #1, *73*
    A Loose Lowered Jaw #2, *73*
    Low Vowels, *74*
    On the Edge, *75–76*
    Paper Towel Tube, *74*
    Pillars of the Throat, *75*
    Posture, *74*
    Rubber Band/Bungee Cord, *75*
    "Stroking the Beard," *74*
resources, 213–226
    Contemporary Commercial Music (CCM), 222–223

Facebook groups/communities, 223–225
iPhone/iPad apps, 226–227
journals, magazines, associations (online), 213–217
musical theater, 221–222
tools for singers, 220–221
vocal health, 218–219

rhythm
coordinating text with, 132–133
memorizing text and, 144–145

rhythmic breathing, 81–82
ring (*squillo*), 36, 53, 89, 101, 121, 156
Rolfing, 148–149
Rubber Band/Bungee Cord, *75*
Rubbing Out the Jaw, *167*
Ruffo, Titta, 123, 160
Rutenberg, Craig, 66

Sacks, Peter, 32
scale, imagery, 65
scooping, 194
self-perception, 29–32
conception and, 28–29
condition hindering self-reflection, 30
Dunning-Kruger effect, 29, 30
Lake Wobegon Effect, 30
narcissism and, 30–32
stages of competence and, 32–33

shadow vowels, 128
Shoot the Pistol, *162*
Shoulder Figure Eights, *166*
Skipping the Rock/Belly Laughing, *93*
soft palate
acoustic cage and, 57
engaging lips and raising, 57–58, 80
exercise for raising, 75
falsetto and, 66
laryngeal collar and raising, 51–52
quick breath before onset and, 86
raised, lowered larynx and, 40, 62–63, 64, 72, 75
resonance and, 40, 41, 62–63
throat position during inhalation, 82–83

song interpretation, attitude/intent and, 34–35
song preparation, 131–139
back to front text prep, 135–137
connecting to core sound in recitative, 137–138
coordinating text with rhythm, 132–133
memorization, 143–145
musical aspects, 132
recurring vowels in text, 138–*139*
stage fright, confidence and, 196
text, 131–137
unwritten rhythms within text, 133–134
working the text, 134–137, 138–139

soprano, 55, 177, 178, 181, 182–183, 184. *See also* vocal registers and range
sotto voce, 66–67
sounds, extraneous, 130–131. *See also* consonants; language; vowels
Spiking the Volleyball, *86–87*
stage fright, 19, 26, 195–197
stage voice, using, 63, 68, *100*, 114, 134, 135, 152
stance, 150. *See also* posture/alignment

Stephens, John, 14, 50, 91
straight tone, 193–194
Straw Technique, *97–98*
"Stroking the Beard," *74*
stuck sound, determining, 65
Sucking Through the Hand and Tending to the Arm, *96–97*
Sundberg, Johan, 44–45, 51

T, words ending with, 128–129
t'ai chi ch'uan, 148
teachers. *See* voice teachers and students
Tennis (Backhand Swing), *92–93*
tenor, 178, 181, 185
tessitura, 55, 183
text. *See also* consonants; language; vowels
   connecting voice to, 111–112
   expressing emotions of, intent/empathy and, 140
   preliminary preparation, 115
   recurring vowels in, 138–139
   relating to, 140
   researching, 141–142
   song preparation, 131–137
   understanding, 139–142
   unwritten rhythms within, 133–134
   working, 134–137, 138–139
   working it like a monologue, 142
theater (musical), resources, 221–222
throat, position during inhalation, 82–83. *See also* larynx; soft palate; vocal tract
Throw the Dart, *162–163*
timbre, 53–54, 183
tone
   focus and placement, 89
   Lamperti on, 41, 50, 51, 78, 84, 87, 89, 151
   levels of onset (glottal/aspirate/coordinated), 84–85
   release of (aspirate/glottal/balanced/flaring), 87–88
tongue
   Gross Chewing, *167*
   position, 60–61
   Relaxing the Jaw and Tongue, *166*
   resonance and, 60–61
   tension, 61
   vowel placement and, 70–71
   warm-ups, *166*, *167*
tools for singers, 220–221. *See also* resources
Trager Approach, 148
tremolo, 193
tuning formants, 44–45
Twenge, Dr. Jean, 31

Unconscious competence, 33
unconscious incompetence, 33
Underwood, Keith, 96–97
unity, 19–20
university, language training, 116–117

Vestibular folds, 52–53
vibrato
   problems (*See* vocal problems, addressing)
   resonance and, 50, 54
   straight tone and, 193–194
   tremolo and, 193
visual memorization, 143–144
vocal disorders and faults, 198–206. *See also* vocal problems, addressing
vocal folds

connecting the cords, 99–103
falling into the breath and, 90
false vocal cords and, 52–53
formants and, 41
International Phonetic
  Alphabet (IPA), 118–120
phonation and, 83–85
timbre and, 53
weight in the voice and, 71–72
vocal fry register, 100–101, 175,
  179, 191, 192
vocal health. *See also* vocal
  problems, addressing
  dos and don'ts, 190–192
  illness, practicing and, 189–190
  resources, 218–219
  vocal disorders and faults,
    198–206
vocal image, 24, 35–36
vocal problems, addressing,
  192–197
  poor choral habits, 194–195
  scooping, 194
  stage fright, 195–197
  straight tone, 193–194
  tremolo, 193
  vibrato imbalance, 192
  vocal disorders and faults,
    198–206
  wobble, 192–193
vocal registers and range. *See also*
  specific registers
  about: perspectives on range,
    175; vocal registers overview,
    176
  chest voice, 177
  Fach system, 182–185
  female registers, 177–178
  head voice, 177–179
  keyboard reference for ranges,
    179

middle voice, 177
mixing registers, 181–182
modal voice, 176–177
number of registers in singing
  voice, 176
register transition, 180–181 (*See
  also passaggio*)
vocal fry register, 100–101, 175,
  179, 191, 192
voice classifications, 182–185
whistle register, 175, 179–180
vocal tract
  falsetto for correct placement,
    66
  formants and (*See* formants)
  resonance and, 46–49 (*See also*
    resonance)
*Vocal Wisdom: Maxims of Giovanni
  Battista Lamperti* (Lamperti), 10
voce di strega, 101, 103
VoceVista, 45
voice. *See also* practicing
  about: this book and, 9–10
  covering and, 69–70
  environment and, 154
  genetics and, 154
  imitating things (*See* imitation)
  mind that sings, instead of, 24
  natural effects on, 153–155
  personalities, resonance and,
    64–65
  playing, 87
  reasons for studying, 8–9
  weight, 71–72, 183
voice teachers and students. *See
  also* practicing; vocal registers and
  range
  AATS teacher guidelines and
    what to look for, 170–174
  about: importance of the
    teacher, 169

INDEX

assessment lesson for prospective student, 174–175
finding the right voice teacher, 169–175
how to find a teacher, 173–174
mechanistic approach, 38
mechanistic approach to teaching, 37
skills teachers should have, 170–172
teachers to avoid, 172–173
teaching approach options, 37–38
wholistic approach to teaching, 37–38
volume, resonance and, 51
vowels, 120–122. *See also* consonants; language; song preparation
  crossover between genres and, 67–69
  exercises, *121–122*, *139*
  formants, 42–44, 120–121
  formants and (*See* formants)
  light-dark (*chiaroscuro*) and, 40, 46, 48, 53, 76, 102
  Low Vowels, *74*
  Modified Vowels, *122*
  placement, 70–71
  pure, engaging, 80
  recurring, in text, 138–*139*
  shadow, 128
  "sweet spot" and, 40
  Working Just the Vowels, *121*

Walking the Table, *109–110*, *164*
The Wall Push, *99*
warm-ups, body, 165–167
  about: overview of, 165, 187
  Bend to the Floor, *166*
  Gross Chewing, *167*
  Head Rolls, *165–166*
  Relaxing the Jaw and Tongue, *166*
  Rubbing Out the Jaw, *167*
  Shoulder Figure Eights, *166*
warm-ups, vocal, 187
website, for related material, 10
weight, voice, 71–72, 183
whistle register, 175, 179–180
wholistic teaching, 37–38
wobble, 192–193
Working Just the Vowels, *121*

ABOUT THE AUTHOR

STANFORD FELIX, DMA, bass-baritone, has performed in opera, concert, and recitals throughout the United States, and has been teaching voice for more than two decades. He received his Bachelor of Fine Arts in Theatre and Voice Performance and Doctor of Musical Arts in Voice Performance from the University of Kansas, Lawrence, and Master of Music degree in Voice Performance from the Manhattan School of Music. He has taught on the voice faculties at Texas A&M University–Kingsville, where he directed and conducted the opera workshop, and Emporia State University in Emporia, Kansas. He founded and was the Musical/Executive Director of Kansas Concert Opera and Minnesota Concert Opera. A composer of choral music and art song, Dr. Felix is a member of the American Composers Forum and National Association of Teachers of Singing (NATS), and former member of the College Music Society. His previous book, *The Complete Idiot's Guide Music Dictionary*, was published by Penguin USA in 2010.

www.ingramcontent.com/pod-product-compliance
Lightning Source LLC
Chambersburg PA
CBHW051050230426
43666CB00012B/2637